JESSE LIVERMORE

Speculator-King

by
PAUL SARNOFF

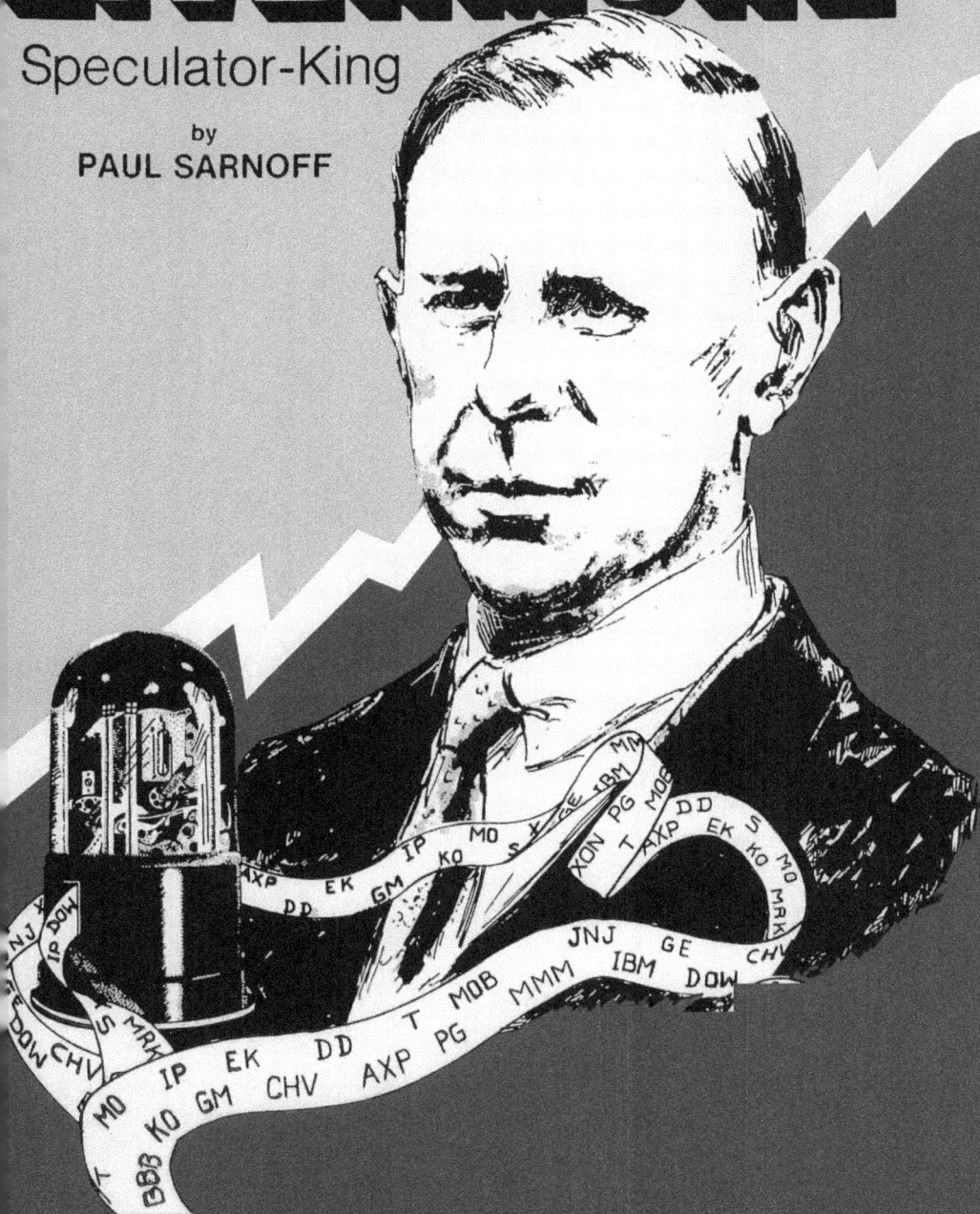

© Copyright 1977 by Paul Sarnoff

Published by Interbooks

CONTENTS

Page

PART I: THE LIVERMORE LUCK 1
WALL STREET WONDER 3
BOY PLUNGER 13
BUCKET-SHOP BAPTISM 21
THE FIRST KILLING 31
COTTON KING 43
THE BIG LEAK 53

PART II: THE LIVERMORE LIFE 61
EVERMORE 63
CUTTEN 75
"J. L." 83
THE JIGGLERS, THE JUGGLERS 93
TWILIGHT BATTLE 107

PART III: THE LIVERMORE LEGACY 115
THE LIVERMORE KEY 117

THE FOUR FACES OF JESSE LIVERMORE 124

BIBLIOGRAPHY 129

ACKNOWLEDGMENTS 131

OTHER BOOKS BY PAUL SARNOFF 132

INDEX 133

PART I

THE LIVERMORE LUCK

"Markets are never wrong; opinions are."
. . . Jesse L. Livermore.

Chapter 1

WALL STREET WONDER

Mid-October, 1929: The world that is Wall Street teeters precariously on the edge of an abyss. The snowball plunge, dead ahead and down, is bound to result in a financial crash whose reverberations will be felt throughout the rest of the world.

For weeks, the market has flashed minor warnings; but the money-hungry public is in high speculative spirits and prefers to ignore the sobering "Caution" signs—whether in print or implied. Here and there, a few wiser heads stop and listen to, even question the ominous rumblings. But the small ripple of their anxious voices is washed aside by the prevailing wave of public optimism.

Saturday, October 18th: The Wall Street world goes over the edge—and starts the devastating downward slide. It is the beginning of one of the worst stock market disasters in all history . . .

In the frenzied two-hour trading session that followed, key stocks broke sharply and roller-coasted to ruin. Anxious brokers gathered on the floor of the Exchange, stricken with fear at the sudden absence of support from the trusts, the pools* and the big buyers like Morgan, Belmont, Rockefeller, Weinberg and others.

The brokerage fraternity, then servicing a margin-

---

*Pools were then legal syndicates, whose money and stock were managed by expert traders or stockbrokers. Each pool sponsored a single issue; and issues supported by well-financed pools could not be broken readily by bear-raiders.

mad public, indeed had plenty to worry about; and the press groped about for an explanation of the coming crash.

In its coverage of that harrowing Saturday session, the Sunday edition of *The New York Times* ran this headline:

Jesse Livermore Reported
To Be Heading Group
Hammering High-Priced
Securities . . .

The page 1, column 1, explanation went on to say that Mr. Livermore, "formerly one of the country's biggest speculators is the leader of the bear clique . . . His attack upon the desperately driven longs (bulls) has caused his profits to run into millions . . ."

Dubbing Livermore "The Wall Street Wonder," the imaginative *Times* writer alluded to the speculator as the "Boy Plunger" who, while still in his teens, had been barred from the Boston bucket-shops*. Singing a paean of praise for Mr. Livermore's stock market sagacity, the reporter eulogized further with: "The memory of his shrewdness and skill in Wall Street has never died . . . Mr. Livermore is the best man on the tape the speculative world has ever known . . ."

Such adulation could hardly escape the notice of Livermore himself, then one of the most loyal fans of *The New York Times.* For him, reading that paper was practically a devotional service at breakfast; and that morning, when Jesse Lauriston Livermore saw his name

---

*Bucket-shops were pseudo-brokerage offices, whose managers settled with the customers strictly on the basis of price fluctuations. A small margin (shoe-string deposit) was put down by the customers. If the market went against them, they were wiped out. When the customers made a killing, the bucket-shops, like Bedouins, folded their operations (without paying off, of course)—and vanished. To be barred from doing business in a bucket-shop was to achieve the height of professional stock market flattery.

—and his reputation—page 1 material again, his slightly cockeyed blue eyes moisted over behind the silver-rimmed spectacles.

But, of course, this particular news story was not true. So to set the record straight (and to keep his name in the *Times*) Mr. Livermore decided to hold a press conference.

The odd thing about this particular "press" conference was that Livermore purposely restricted his invitation to the *Times.* Perhaps he sensibly realized that other newspapers would quickly lift whatever information he gave to the *Times* and spread it all over the country. This turned out to be precisely the case.

On the morning of October 21, 1929, the reporter from *The New York Times* entered the lobby of the Heckscher Building (730 Fifth Avenue, New York City) and walked quickly to the elevator marked "Penthouse."

As he ascended to what was then "the most luxurious office in New York," he found himself recalling bits and pieces of the Livermore legend:

. . . It was rumored that Mr. Livermore, twice-married and the father of two sons, was seeking a divorce . . . It was well-known that Mr. Livermore rode only in Rolls-Royces and owned at least a half-dozen residences (summer and winter homes) . . . It was observed and reported that the fabulous Livermore, who drank like a fish, could make and lose millions as effortlessly as he downed martinis; that he was a sucker for any pretty girl; that he loved to gamble in the market more than he loved anything else in the world. His own customer's man testified that when "Mr. Livermore was gambling he was thinking of screwing; when he was screwing he was thinking of gambling" . . . Jealous colleagues in the Wall Street jungle pooh-poohed Livermore's assertion that he was a 60-40 player, happy to make his millions on the 20%. They assessed him as an over-rated charlatan, a failure—sometimes right with other people's money, but usually wrong with his own.

Oddly enough, there was a measure of truth to these reports. Jesse Livermore indeed had gone bankrupt several times. What made him such a wonder on Wall Street was that every time he went broke it was stockbrokers who were his creditors; and more wondrous still, these same hard-hearted creditors always readily absolved him from his debts! Presumably, the answer might be found in Livermore's widely publicized reputation for eventually paying his creditors every cent he owed them; but the rumor that the brokers couldn't afford to have him out of action in view of the immense commissions he generated would appear to be a far more plausible explanation.

In fact, the *Times* once reported trader Livermore had made a million dollars in one day selling thousands of shares of stock short, while evening himself out nicely on the very same day by losing a cool million in his long position on Cotton! Oh, yes . . . it was hard to tell who loved Livermore more—the newspapers to whom he was always good copy, the brokers he fattened, or the army of spies, runners, and other minions he kept greasing for dependable inside information supposed to steer him to profits.

No wonder the *Times* writer was so excited at the prospect of covering this flamboyant personage. What sort of man would he be, this "Master Spirit in the World of Stock Market Speculation?" Well, the reporter would soon find out; for Livermore's secretary, a silent, soft-footed man, was now escorting him into the inner sanctum of the Great Presence.

At first, the *Times* man felt as though he stood before the Dalai Lama . . . Sphinxlike, imperturbable and rigid

—there sat Jesse Livermore, behind a huge mahogany desk, whose surface shone scrupulously bare. The famous speculator hardly acknowledged the newsman's entry. Instead, he reached for the telephone resting on a ledge to his left, and carefully covering the mouthpiece with his delicate fingers, began to whisper market orders to an unidentified ally, somewhere deep in the financial district. While Livermore was busy murmuring instructions into the phone, the reporter had a chance to look him over.

At fifty-two, Jesse Livermore appeared to be at least ten years younger. Slim and slight of build, his hands were almost womanly in slenderness and smoothness. On his right pinky finger, he wore a huge sapphire in a setting designed for the masculine hand. The morning sun reflected in the stone, which blazed like a baleful eye. His hair, shot through with tell-tale patches of frost, was still predominantly blond; it ran straight back from a high forehead, somewhat bald at the sides and formed a formidable crest above his face. His generous nose supported *pince-nez* glasses. The eyes were blue, with an owlish stare like that of a professor absorbed with some knotty problem.

All in all, Jesse Livermore presented a picture of a cultured, well-dressed man. His double-breasted suit of banker's grey was cut from finest quality cloth— and expensively tailored. He wore a spotless white shirt with the new lay-down collar, from whose innards a costly red foulard snaked down the precise center of his shirt to disappear under the vee of his vest. Across Livermore's chest hung a delicate gold chain of simple links. Its ends were hidden in his vest-pockets. The reporter couldn't help wondering what might be hanging from each end of the chain. As if reading the newsman's mind, Livermore cradled the ear-piece on his shoulder and fished out a slim gold pencil hanging from one end of the chain. The ever-present secretary automatically slid a pad of paper before his boss who quickly covered the pad with coded markings.

Suddenly, Livermore tucked the pencil back into his vest-pocket, cradled the receiver back onto its hook, and yanked out a little gold knife, attached to the other end of his chain. "The Great Bear" twisted the knife nervously between his fingers . . . and now—for the first time—turned his attention to the waiting reporter.

The change was almost magical — With a warm, friendly smile crinkling up the corners of his eyes, Livermore welcomed the newsman with a cordial wave toward a barrel-chair nearby. "The Speculator-King" did not offer to shake hands. He never did—with anyone; he abhorred physical contact with any male (although females were another story). Carefully controlling his agitation (Livermore was "quick, nervous and excitable"), he tried to look patient as he awaited the inquisition.

The fact was, Jesse Livermore had little patience—or liking—for anything but the exciting war-game of winning profits from price changes. His warfare—the thrill of beating his fellow man—was confined solely to the marketplace. What made the marketplace so fascinating to him was his unshakeable conviction that *there* success could be consistently won on a basis other than sheer luck. Moreover, from the time he was a boy, Mr. Livermore had labored diligently toward the perfection of a scientific "key" to stock market success. As yet, he had not succeeded in finding this elusive key.

"Success rides on the hour of decision," he preached to his few confidants; and by the third week in October, 1929, he indeed had made his decision. Prices of issues, compared to their values, were far too high. This could lead to only one natural end. And so, deliberately, Mr.

Livermore was then heavily short of the market.

The speculator's face was enigmatic as he sat waiting for the reporter to speak. Obviously, there would be no ice-breaking niceties. On with the questions then:

"Is it true, Mr. Livermore, that you are the leader of the bear clique?"

The man alluded to as Daniel Drew's successor answered by reaching into a desk-drawer, fishing out a single sheet of neatly-typed paper, and passing it to the newsman—without a word.

Not knowing whether to shove the paper into his pocket or to read it, the puzzled reporter ventured, "Aren't you going to answer my question?"

"Look," Livermore replied in a hushed voice ripping the air like a stiletto, "your paper accused me of raiding the market. My written reply proves my innocence. Read it. Then I'll answer your questions."

And the reporter read:

> In connection with the various reports . . . indiscriminately spread during the past few days through the newspapers and various brokerage houses to the effect that a large bear pool has been formed supervised by myself and financed by various well-known capitalists, I wish to state that there is no truth whatever in any such rumors as far as I am concerned and I know of no combinations having been formed by others . . .

Here, the reporter paused and looked up to ask, "But Mr. Livermore, why are stocks going down?" And the obliging speculator, as if speaking for other stock market manipulators of the past, said succinctly, "What has happened . . . is the inevitable result of continuous, rank manipulation of many stock issues to prices many times their actual worth based upon real earnings and yield returns . . . If anyone will take the trouble to analyze the prices of . . . stocks . . . they must look at them as selling at ridiculously high prices . . ."

Having unburdened himself of this trenchant statement, Mr. Livermore pushed back against his padded swivel-chair, while twirling the little pen-knife furiously between his ever-moving fingers.

"But Mr. Livermore," the *Times* man prodded, "Professor Fisher (of Yale) claims that stocks are cheap. Isn't that the way most people feel about the market?"

For a moment, Livermore's eyes burned angrily. "Professor Fisher!" he snorted; "What can a professor know about speculation or stock markets! Did he ever trade on margin? Does he have a single cent in any of those bubbles he thinks are cheap?"

Without waiting for answers, Livermore then continued his lecture: "You must beware of inside information —all inside information. Since this is true, how can the public possibly rely on information coming from a classroom? I tell you the market never stands still. It acts like the ocean. There are waves of accumulation and distribution. The market always tells you when you are wrong; so let's leave it to the market to tell its own story—with or without help from college professors."

But the newsman was persistent; he was not going to be fobbed off with just a prepared statement and a few cliché-ridden generalities. He was there to get some specifics, so he asked, "Are you not on the short side since you believe the market will break?"

Livermore's answer was quick and glib—and a lie: "What little I do in the market has always been as an individual and will continue to be on such a basis. It is very foolish to think that any individual could artificially bring about a decline in the stock market in a country so large and so prosperous as the United States . . . Let me say that while I believe many stocks will go down, the market will always contain bargains."

Naturally, Livermore had not answered the reporter's question satisfactorily at all; but his reference to "bargains" gave the young writer his cue. "How do you find these bargains?" he asked.

"Right now," the master speculator said with a smile, "that little secret is *my* business—and is not for publication." Then with an imperious wave, he sent the reporter packing.

On the way down in the elevator—in fact, all the way back to the *Times*—the newsman asked himself:

> . . . Is Livermore telling the truth? Is he the leader of the bears? How deep is he on the short side? Does he own anything long? Is it true that he has a secret board-room with thirty telephones and twenty clerks, including board-boys to chalk up the ever-changing prices? Is he acting for other manipulators? Is he in cahoots with Whitney, Baruch, Block, Hutton? Could the country-wide rumors be true that "Livermore's on a raid" . . . "Livermore's out to ruin the country" . . .?

Not knowing whether the speculator had been candid in the interview or was actually hiding the truth, the reporter started to write his column. Its headline began: "Mr. Livermore's Sentiments."

What really *were* Mr. Livermore's sentiments? How did this sphinx-like operator fare financially during the week-long crash that followed—and the ensuing, long, worrisome years of national depression? How did he come to be publicly charged with leading the stock market to ruin? And why do most people still believe he was one of the most successful speculators who ever lived, while others believe his life—in private and in the market—reflected mostly failure?

To examine this American's bizarre past, it is best to start at the beginning: July 26, 1877.

Chapter 2

BOY PLUNGER

On that day, in Shrewsbury, Massachusetts, a son was born to Laura (Prouty) and Hiram E. Livermore. The proud, but poor, parents promptly named the babe Jesse Lauriston.

Jesse's coming could hardly be called propitious. His father, a plain-dirt farmer, could barely scrape an existence out of the rock-riddled fields; indeed, the country itself still staggered from the wake of the great panic of 1873. Money—specie, that is—appeared to be virtually non-existent, and the Livermores sought life's necessities through the barter system. Father Livermore just happened to be a failure as a farmer, and he lost the place at Shrewsbury before young Jesse even reached the toddler stage. The family was then obliged to move into grandfather Livermore's farm-house at Paxton. There, Hiram Livermore labored for several years until he had saved enough from his laborer's "wages" to set down a payment on a homestead at South Acton.

In New England in the 19th Century, work—especially for the plain-dirt farmer—proved to be unduly wearing. The main reason, of course, lay in the rock-strewn fields.

Before Jesse was old enough to read, he busily followed his father's plow-horse, lifting the rocks unearthed by the blade and lugging them over to be neatly piled as part of the fences rimming the fields. It seemed quite natural for farmer Livermore to hope his son would grow strong, and take to the farmwork. But as Jesse approached his teens, his father's hopes began to fade like a winter sunset.

Thin, frail, and sick a good part of the time, young Jesse turned hungrily to the few books and sparse educational material dispensed by the town of Acton's school. By his own admission, he became a "whiz at mathematics." But his greatest pleasure centered upon devouring the occasional newspapers arriving at the Livermore homestead. This became a compulsory habit for the rest of his life.

Young Jesse was gifted with an inordinately active imagination; and he quickly realized—by reading Boston papers—that there existed indeed an easier life than the one his parents suffered. The life he read about promised luxury, beautiful women, music—and fame.

With the same decisive stubbornness typifying his later stock market speculations, Jesse resolved to set out and win not only the luxury and the money for "the good life" but—more important—fame.

Pragmatically, he realized he could never be famous if he, like his father, followed a plow-horse on a Massachusetts plot to the end of his days. So he promptly made plans to leave home. But he was merely a slip of a boy—aged twelve going on twenty.

According to the custom of that time, the father, of course, acted as head of the house. He usually made the important decisions. Coddling youngsters, especially among the poor, was unthinkable; and Hiram Livermore's youngster was no exception. He had little time for his son; so whatever love or attention the boy received came from his mother. Jesse shrewdly decided to employ his mother in his plan to escape. Patiently, and with the surreptitious scheming which later made him the terror of the marketplace, young Jesse bided his time. Deep down inside, he crooned over and over— a song of hope, of ambition: "I'm going to be rich. I'm going to be famous. Someday I'm going to give my Ma a thousand dollars . . ."

A thousand dollars! Just about all the money in the world to a young farmboy, who had yet to handle a dollar of his own. But Jesse, once determined, went through each day saying, "Someday . . ."

That "someday" took time—and a lot of doing. And it was Jesse's father who inadvertently speeded its arrival.

Shortly after the boy's fourteenth birthday, Farmer Livermore told him he had had enough schooling, and it was high-time he donned overalls and lent a hand at home—full-time, that is. Jesse overtly acceded to his father's demand; but covertly, he considered another idea, one long harbored in his brain.

And so before his hands ever got to raise the inevitable calluses, young Jesse ran away from home.

Fortified with small financial assistance from his mother (and telling his father nothing), Jesse simply meandered out onto the Boston pike on a sunny day in 1891 and hopped onto a friendly wagon heading for the city.

As the wagon rumbled over the road into Boston, Jesse experienced not one regret at having run away; nor did he worry about what his parents might feel or think. Often, he had revealed to his mother his grandiose plans and dreams of wealth, of fame and power. But Ma Livermore usually clucked at his boyish ravings and turned back to the butter-churn or the milk-pail.

Oh, yes . . . Jesse's pattern was emerging—and it was one he was to live by for the rest of his life.

Apparently, the moment he abandoned something, he could drop it as though it had never existed. And in this instance, was it not understandable? After all, he now had the personal and immediate worry of making ends meet, of keeping body and soul alive so he could make those hoped-for millions. Oddly enough, in *this* area, Jesse's confidence was supreme and absolute.

This boy of fourteen, on his lone way to the big city for the first time in his life, counted even then upon the kindness of strangers. He knew with the instinct of a born confidence-man that people are always suckers for young boys just turning into men—especially boys with clear, candid faces, honest blue eyes, straw-blond hair, and a toothsome grin, to boot.

He was so right.

Hopping down from the wagon on Milk Street, he strode confidently into the office of Paine Webber and asked to see "the partner."

It might be fun to conjecture about just what this hay-seedy-looking lad, fresh from the farm, actually said to the Paine Webber partner . . . but it wouldn't be history. Perhaps he simply blurted out he didn't want to use his hands solely to raise blisters on his palms, when he could be using the excellent brain in his head.

In any event—and just like in fairy tales—the impoverished runaway suddenly found himself hired by one of Boston's leading brokerage firms, as a board-boy at $6 a week.

Appearing older than his years, Jesse rented a room in a nearby boarding-house, got some second-hand clothes, and reported to work.

A person with good manners, he thought—even though he may not advance—at least doesn't offend; he, therefore, assumed an extremely polite approach to his fellow chalkers-of-changing-prices. It wasn't long before he became as much a fitting of the board-room as the ticker itself.

Every business day, after breakfast, Jesse would rush out of the boarding-house, literally dash to the office in the hope of being the first person at the front door. Possibly, he had read something about the early bird's becoming financially fat; at any rate, he often had to wait fifteen or twenty minutes until a partner arrived with the door-key. And as soon as he stepped over the threshold, Jesse removed his jacket, donned an alpaca office-coat, and cleaned off the boards. Naturally, his diligence did not escape notice.

In those days—long, long before today's electronic quotation devices—everything depended upon the slender, ecru tape spilling out of a bell-jarred stock-ticker. Usually, a knowledgeable customer parked himself next to the ticker, picked up the moving tape, and called off the changing prices to board-boys like Jesse.

Quickly, the boys would erase existing prices and chalk the changes on enormous blackboards lining the brokerage office wall. Thus, customers in this "board-room" could look up from their seats (or standing positions, in crowded places) and see the *last sale* in stocks, bonds or commodities.

The clack of the ticker, the piercing voices crying out prices, the back-and-forth rush to order clerk or cage (cashier's window)—all of it gave Jesse such an inward lift that he knew the brokerage business could readily satisfy anybody's—especially his—craving for action.

In the beginning, the prices he so ardently chalked up on the blackboards meant little more than nothing to young Livermore. He had all he could do to catch changes from the tape-caller and post them properly under the right security after erasing previous prices. There was no time to wonder about what these prices, or their changes, represented. It wasn't long, however, before he learned.

Sponge-like, he sopped up all the board-room gossip his ears happened to catch, devoured the financial pages and examined the tout-sheet tacked to the office bulletin-board; and like a sponge, he never gave of himself unless he was squeezed.

Although he appeared to be getting along successfully, Jesse was far short, of course, of his ultimate goal —to become someday, somehow, a multi-millionaire. "Conceive an idea," was his theory, "then stick to it. Only those who hang on are ever worthwhile . . ."

Once he became familiar with the workings of the business he found himself in, he concluded he had found the right road to those millions; now he could concentrate on pursuing it. He had started his business life in the market; there he was going to stay—and find his millions. In short, he decided that—in view of his irrevocable dedication to the market—it *owed* him a living.

Jesse knew that in order to reach his ambitious destination, he would have to have a campaign. The first real milestone had to be: an important enough sum of money to work with; so how could he set about attaining it? To begin with, there were two "musts": to become well-known, and to develop a "fool-proof" stock market system.

The system would have to remain in limbo for the time being because Jesse's initial energies were being applied to the business of making himself well-known. He began to drop "points" (tips). "From the facts," he would whisper confidentially to a board-room habitué, "Steel is due for a rise." And when confronted with the natural reaction, "How do you know?"—Jesse's answer was, *"They* say so . . . " ("They," of course, being those mysterious, often non-existent people always "in the know").

Fortunately for young Jesse, some of his "points" worked out well. He began to be liked by his fellow-workers, as well as the hangers-on in the brokerage office. This sudden fine feeling of importance unleashed something inside him; he warmed to his popularity with the joy of a half-frozen lamb in a winter blizzard on being carried in and set before a farmer's fire. Indeed, Jesse Livermore—in his own opinion, at least—began to consider himself an *authority*. "He *knew*," people said, "how to pick stocks."

This fillip to his ego worked wonders. It created a permanent euphoria in Jesse Livermore's make-up that not even three future bankruptcies could dispel. He became cocky.

One day, about a year after he had been in Boston, Jesse was accosted by an envious board-boy, who said, "If you're so good at picking winners, why don't you put your money where your mouth is?"

Struggling to subdue his temper, Jesse calmly countered with, "I don't care about the money. It's being *right* that counts."

"But if you're right, you can get rich," continued his tormentor.

This sentence changed Jesse's life. The challenge hit him like a mule-kick, and he was never the same. Then and there, he began to think about trying his luck, for now he reasoned the clear and easy road to riches simply lay in the direction of being *right* about the direction of a stock's price—and doing something about it! Simple? Well, so it seemed to a young man nearing sixteen, who had been closely looking at price changes in the stock market for slightly less than a year.

Construing Jesse's silence to be a sign of cowardice, the nuisance (who inadvertently supplied the key to the stock market vault for Jesse Livermore) barked, "Well?"

Jesse looked flatly into his heckler's eyes and said, "Thanks for the thought. When I'm ready, I'll use it—and I'm going to get rich when I'm ready, too."

Just after his sixteenth birthday, Jesse decided he was ready. On one of his days off, he went with a friend to a bucket-shop in Worcester and risked "ten dollars on Burlington." The enterprising pair quickly cleared $3.12 each. This first profit—this insignificant prize—launched the farm boy (remembered for all time as the "Boy Plunger") on his legendary stock market career.

When Jesse's boss at Paine Webber found out his employee made a habit of frequenting bucket-shops, he sternly warned the ambitious young gambler to stay out of "those dens of iniquity, or else."

Jesse chose the "or else" alternative, and promptly found himself fired from the first, the only, job he ever held.

There appeared to be only one thing he could do now. Because he hadn't sufficient capital to trade in regular brokerage offices, Jesse Livermore—feeling like St. George on his way to slay the dreaded dragon—set out to "take the bucket-shops."

Chapter 3

BUCKET-SHOP BAPTISM

In 1893, the better bucket-shops in Boston—just like their counterparts throughout the country—appeared to be just like offices of member firms of the New York Stock Exchange: complete with tickers, bulletins, and board-boys. There was a vast difference, however, in their operating methods.

Exchange members accepted buy and sell orders for their clients, and handed them "reports" (notices that the trades had actually occurred) when the actual shares in question were either bought or sold. On the other hand, bucket-shops settled trades with their clients simply by using Stock Exchange (or Commodity Exchange) prices as a guide.

For example, when a minor plunger entered an order to buy 100 Copper at $90 a share in a bucket-shop, he was handed an "execution" as soon as the shares of Copper showed up on the ticker at $90. If the stock rose to, say, $94, the fortunate "gambler" could "close out the trade" (or "sell" the shares he actually hadn't bought) as soon as a *real* trade at $94 ran across the tape.

Of course, in trading through a Stock Exchange firm, a speculator attempting to duplicate the above couldn't buy Copper at $90 unless a bona fide *seller* appeared at that level to convey the stock. Conversely, the speculator—if he did buy at $90—couldn't sell his shares at $94 unless there appeared a bona fide buyer at that level, to take the shares off his hands.

But Jesse, carrying a slim bankroll, wasn't affluent enough to worry just yet about how to beat the fellows on the floor of the Exchange. Gifted with sharp eyes, a ready ear, and the speed of a striking rattlesnake, Jesse believed he could slap down his buy and sell tickets fast enough at any bucket-shop cage to "scalp" some points every day.

This young, under-capitalized speculator, when trading in the bucket-shops, was able to enjoy another obvious advantage. Not only did he have to put down less of a deposit (margin) than he would at a member firm, but if the market declined and he was "wiped out" (lost his deposit), the loss was restricted to the extent of his "bet." He already knew that trading through Exchange firms could result in larger losses—as well as law-suits, if margin calls (demands for further security for the broker) were not met and the client became sold out with a loss in excess of his deposit. Jesse (then a bullish speculator) knew, therefore, when he set out to beat the Boston bucket-shops that should there be a market drop, he couldn't lose more than he risked.

In *Remininscences of a Stock Market Operator* (recently reprinted by TRADERS PRESS, INC.), author E. LeFevre describes in minute detail the bucket-shop baptism of a supposedly fictional plunger named Larry Livingston. Just before his death in 1940, Jesse Livermore revealed that he had actually penned this book (in which he called himself "Livingston"), and that Le-Fevre, a skilled writer, had acted as editor and coach.

In any event, Livingston's—or Livermore's—baptism in these active betting-palaces is so well described in that entertaining book, that a second-rate account here would not do it justice. The book claims that Livermore managed to "take the bucket-shops" so effectively, he became "banned in Boston."

At that time, being banned from trading in a bucket-shop was tantamount to the highest degree of flattery for any speculator. Literally drunk with success at his banishment, Livermore (according to LeFevre) confidently tackled Wall Street—intent on cleaning up in the market.

His first attempt at a killing, however, back-fired. For the highly successful raider of the "buckateers" now entered what was for him a new world, about which he had much to learn: "stock ahead" (an order isn't executed at a specific price although it is printed so on the tape—meaning someone else's order has hit the floor first); "matched and lost" (orders arriving simultaneously at a post on the floor, with insufficient stock available at a specific price, are executed according to the flip of a coin) and the arena of the "late tape" (during periods of activity, trades printed on the tape may be five to ten minutes behind actual trades on the floor and the speculator cannot demand an execution even though he sees the price on the tape go through his limit).

It didn't take the forerunners of today's specialists very long to strip Jesse Livermore. He blamed his losses, of course, on not being able to follow tape-action.

At that time, Jesse, in fact, worshipped the tape. "You can't fool the tape," he claimed, "but it can surely fool you . . ." A chastened, sobered, and financially flattened "tapeworm" rode sadly out of New York in a box-car and went West—to Indianapolis, Chicago, St. Louis, and to Denver—in order to scalp a living from the stock betting-palaces, where the customers had five hours—from "ten-to-three"—to cheer their choices, compared to the customary three minutes for selections at the track.

By 1900, Livermore, then twenty-three, somehow had amassed a roll approximating $50,000. True to his word, he returned home to fulfill his youthful promise and gave his Ma a thousand dollars. And he brought with him still another prize—his wife. For during his country-wide—and seven-year assault—on the bucket-shops, Jesse had fallen in love with and married an Indianapolis girl, Nettie Jordan.

"Being broke is a very efficient educational agency," Jesse observed, "and I never liked, or enjoyed, being broke. I wanted to make big money, and the only place big money was was Wall Street. I promised myself I'd beat those boys at their own game, even if I had to buy a seat to do it . . ."

As it turned out, of course, he never became sacrosanct enough for the Exchange's Board of Governors to clear his application. But at twenty-three, Jesse—happy with his first wife, and well-heeled with bucket-shop winnings—daringly returned to Wall Street for another try. Young and cocky as he appeared, he did have something to boast about: the money and experience gained in his seven-year joust with the bucketeers.

Under his facade of supreme confidence, however, the young man constantly flayed himself with doubt. He just couldn't reconcile his uncanny ability to skin the skinners in the bucket-shops with his apparent inability to beat the boys trading on the floor of the Exchange. And this he became determined to do—with all the dedication of a Buddhist monk. Now was the time for him to start thinking seriously about a *system* . . .

Obviously, he reasoned, tape-trading could hardly work effectively in attacking brokers in a favored position on the floor. He had to be able to envision price moves *before* they occurred.

Predicting prices in Wall Street has always offered the same challenge to the venturesome that finding the touchstone to turn lead into gold once held to alchemists. For a while, Livermore studied the methods of one of the first market technicians, a Frenchman. But he soon realized that charts can't tell a trader what the board of directors of a company might do. He did, however, attribute some modicum of importance to examination of the past price movements of a stock issue. Little by little, Livermore began to learn "the essential difference between betting on price fluctuations and anticipating advances and declines." He found the "touchstone" that made the difference between gambling and speculating—something we today call "research."

Simply put, research—especially when it refers to the market—is reliable information. Livermore began to seek authentic information. He began to learn that prices are not made by earnings or by dividends, but rather by *people.* He listened to success and failure stories of the legendary operators. He began to learn all he could about manipulating market prices. Most of all, he saw at first-hand the awesome power of a press release to influence the course of the market price of any specific stock. He learned to gauge which way prices would go when news of national import reached the floor of the Exchange. As he learned, he won and he lost. But, at the same time, he *lived.*

Summers, he maintained a cottage at Long Branch, on the Jersey Shore. There he mixed with affluent capitalists and financiers—always listening, *always* learning.

He seldom entered into conversation, but was scrupulous about observing the amenities. Winters, he lived with his childless bride at the fashionable Windsor Hotel on Fifth Avenue. "The more I made," he confessed, "the more I spent." He admitted to friends, "I don't want to die disgustingly rich . . ."

He may not have wanted to die that way; but apparently that's the way he wanted to live. And he tried to do it by winning tellingly in the perennial war between the bulls and the bears—a war that began in 1836, when Jacob Little invented the short sale. From that time on, owners of stock could sell their shares on the Exchange; and speculators, who didn't own any stock at all found themselves able to sell stock they didn't own, in the hope of replacing the short shares (delivered temporarily by their brokers to the buyers) with new shares purchased at lower prices. Thus, a speculator feeling Copper at $95 was too high promptly sold, say, 100 shares short. His broker lent him the shares at the $95-level for delivery to the buyer, and the speculator (acting as a bear) prayed for the price of Copper to drop, so he could go into the market, buy 100 shares at, say, $80—and replace the shares he had borrowed at the $95-level—pocketing the difference, after commissions.

The speculator, like Livermore, thus found himself in an intriguing market, one in which he not only could sell stock he already owned, but also stock he didn't own, but could borrow. Simply speaking, Livermore realized that just as he stood to make $100 on each point of market rise for every 100 shares of stock he owned (on which he was long), so did he stand to profit by $100 a point for every point of market decline in the price of shares he was short (had borrowed).

Wall Street has always been a two-way street. Jesse Livermore didn't care which way it went as long as it fluctuated. He prepared himself to make money whichever way the market moved. First, he searched for value (stocks trading at a price representing a substantial discount from where they should have been selling). And he sought to position these issues. Then he searched for over-priced stocks to sell short.

In this way, he achieved passable success for several years. On balance, he made money from this period of trial speculation in his search for an effective system. "Speculation is not an easy business," he later said. "It is not a game for the stupid, the mentally lazy, the man of inferior emotional balance . . ."

Oh, yes—Jesse Livermore in 1901, could hardly be excluded from the roster of those shrewd speculators who generally manage to subsist for a time through a series of quick small-profit moves. But he did throw money to the winds rather recklessly.

In a typical display of self-advertisement, he "leaked" to the newspapers that he had just returned from a European trip during which he had purchased for his wife $12,000 worth of jewelry. Because the Livermores had failed to declare the duty on this purchase, they were clobbered for $7,200 by the Customs officers. Then Jesse made an understandable mistake . . .

He had no sooner deposited his wife and the steamer-trunks at the hotel, when he rushed down to Wall Street to recoup the cost of his recent trip (plus the financial indignity his bank account suffered at government hands).

Barely examining the stock list, Livermore hastily concluded stocks had soared far too high for comfort during his absence. Blindly, and without first checking the economic reasons for the rise, he plunged heavily into the short side of the market.

As stocks continued to rise, friendly brokers (those who looked upon Livermore as a commission generator) cautioned him to hedge by going long. Others urged him to cover (close out his abortive short position). But when Livermore believed he was right, he was as bull-headed as they come.

Bull-headedness can be the curse (though in some cases, the blessing) of great men; for Livermore, trying to attain greatness, it meant going broke. Failing to meet margin-calls, he was "bought-in."*

On the jolting hack-ride uptown after he had been flattened out (left with a zero-balance at the brokers), Livermore agonizingly reviewed his mistakes. He became painfully aware of one simple truism, he had ignored: "Never buck a trend . . ." It was surprising, indeed, that an experienced operator like Livermore had been almost ruined by turning his back on this basic tenet.

Mrs. Livermore, however, still had the "family jewels." It came as quite a shock to Nettie that her huband had gone so wrong in the market he had to ask her to hock her jewels to bankroll a new start. She refused. And to all intents and purposes, their brief happiness ended right there. Livermore threw some shirts and socks in a bag and left. What happened to Nettie wasn't revealed by the record.

Meanwhile, highly confident he could lick the action in the bucket-shops, Livermore traveled all over New England, scalping out a meager living as he went. Those who knew him by reputation immediately refused to honor his orders; so he simply switched to an alias, "Jesse Lord."

Jokingly, word went around the board-rooms in Boston that "Lord Livermore" just happened to be a foolish fellow, who could readily scalp stock market betting-parlors for a few dollars, but just couldn't crack the safe for the "big swing" down in New York.

---

*When a short-seller fails to deposit needed margin, the broker enters the market, buys shares to replace those already borrowed and debits the speculator for the market difference (plus buy-commissions). Often this buying to "cover shorts" creates a still higher surge in the list. Invariably, after the shorts have covered, the list temporarily declines.

And then a suave, highly literate stock-promoter in Boston became intensely interested in Jesse Livermore. This manipulator's name was Thomas W. Lawson.

Chapter 4

THE FIRST KILLING

Boston Lawson (the sobriquet by which he has been immortalized) happened to be one of those minor meteors that emerges intermittently in all ages to flash briefly across stock market skies. He was one of those brilliant operators who burn themselves out quickly because of unforeseen circumstances. The pattern is always the same: speedy success, a legendary reputation —and then ruin. In the case of Thomas Lawson, he later kept the wolf from his wine-cellar by dipping into his lurid memories and penning sensational exposés.*

It was in the handful of years following the turn of the century that Boston Lawson earned his reputation for exerting a modest influence on stock price movements —even though the major portion of his stunning successes involved outright manipulation.

Lawson's *modus operandi* required his having a "front" man; and so, in the fall of 1905, he sent for Livermore. He knew the "tragedy" gnawing away at Livermore—his inability to live "in style," the style he so loved. Moreover, Lawson correctly assumed Livermore owed several very trusting souls in the brokerage business several thousands of dollars. Lawson also was aware, of course, that Livermore's reputation with "the fellers on the floor" in New York City was that of a born loser—a loser, that is, in correctly guessing the direc-

---

*See: *Frenzied Finance*, and *The High Cost of Living*, by Thomas W. Lawson.

tion of prices. And Lawson realized that if he used Livermore for a front (nominee), he could readily begin an operation without showing his hand.

Traditionally, great stock market operators of the past have been most successful when the floor-traders were lulled into believing them to be inactive. The chances for success (in the days of manipulation before the SEC) were even better if sophisticated traders at the Exchange believed the front to be foolish, and without resources.

So it proved to be, when Jesse Livermore returned to the paper arena for another tilt with the "pros." This time, however, he did not act for himself, but as an agent for Lawson. Under the unwritten code of the Street, a non-broker agent acts strictly for his principal, and doesn't "get in the way" (make similar transactions for his own account while executing his benefactor's orders).

Shortly after Livermore again appeared in New York's financial district, he approached some of the brokers with whom he had dealt in the past, put up Lawson's money—and began to "go right." It wasn't too long before board-room Doubting Thomases forgot Livermore's previous failures, as if they had never happened. Livermore's shrewd, but muted, campaign of self-advertisement soon reached the ears of affluent businessmen, who every once in a while took "flyers" in the market; and he became the much-admired target of several traders, who urged him to handle accounts for other plungers, who were convinced Livermore had a better feel of the market than they had. Acting for these anonymous, self-aggrandizing souls, the traders offered Jesse deals ranging from ten to twenty per cent of profits he secured—with no liability for losses incurred.

To Livermore, this sounded asinine. Unbeknown to

his supplicants, he already had committed himself to just such a deal with a Boston "friend." Jesse accurately understood that the road to a stock market fortune did not lie in the direction of making profits for other people. Usually, the trouble isn't worth the wear on the advisor's nerves; and, invariably, the share received doesn't compensate for that trouble. So he wisely made a counter-offer.

Admittedly, his offer wasn't original, or even unique; but it was one that always proved to be effective. To sum it up, the money-man put up the funds, and Livermore did the trading. And as soon as cumulated profits in the account equalled the original risk, Livermore became a partner. From that time on, the account was split fifty-fifty.

Just such an arrangement was put into effect (through a New York broker) with Livermore and an anonymous client, in the early part of spring, 1906.

Naturally, Livermore hadn't bothered to tell Lawson about his trading for others. He figured, Lawson could hardly find out about it anyway. In the meantime, he was duty-bound to look after Lawson's interests.

At first Livermore made several probing trades for his "partnership" account—bad guesses resulting in small losses.

"Take small losses and let profits run," he was reputed to have said later, when he was considered to be an authority on methods of speculating. He emphatically advised his listeners: "You must learn to take losses"—but it was advice he himself always found bitter to swallow.

And then, in March, Boston Lawson instructed Livermore to let out a line of short sales in Union Pacific. Without hesitation, Livermore followed his principal's orders; but one of his pressing hunches urged him to commit the major portion of his partnership account to a similar maneuver in the *same* stock.

The pool in UP (and in those days of scanty regulation they were actually the manipulators of the issue) quickly noticed that someone seemed foolhardy enough to "raid their stock" (try to break down the market by short-selling). Gleefully, they permitted Jesse Livermore to come in easily. As the price of Union Pacific began to rise—slowly and inexorably—the trap cocked itself. Livermore, his Boston client, and his New York City partner were all headed dangerously on the course to financial ruin as he stubbornly kept going short of UP, in the rising market. Of course, on the Exchange floor, the pool-buyers knew that, if they demanded delivery, Livermore couldn't possibly deliver the shares he kept selling short. They sat back licking their chops in anticipation of the forthcoming financial disaster for those reckless bears raiding their issue.

"I can't tell you why I kept shorting Union Pacific," Livermore admitted; but he added boldly, "I wasn't worried a bit . . ."

Maybe he wasn't worried; but his brokers were. They demanded more margin—but settled instead for Livermore's smooth promises. Summoning all the carefully and cunningly cultivated braggadocio he had acquired in his jousts with bucket-shops, Livermore assured his brokers money soon would be forthcoming "from the North" (meaning Boston).

Meanwhile, Livermore's New York partner began to fidget uncomfortably. "It's perfectly fine for you to sit tight as Union Pacific goes up;" he complained, "you have nothing to lose; but I stand to lose a fortune . . ."

"You're wrong," Livermore replied coldly; "I have much more than you to lose. I can be *wrong*."

Being wrong about one of his market plays was, to

Livermore, always more distressing than actual loss of capital. Money hadn't the value for him it had for Russell Sage, who once said, "Any man can earn a dollar, but it takes a wise man to keep it . . ."

In this regard at least, Livermore may be considered a total failure as a wise man. To him, money served only two major functions: first and foremost, to prove he was *right* about the market; and second, to spend for *living.* He never became a hoarder, and every time he hit the market right, and a fortune rained into his ready hands he used it to enjoy life.

In the case of Livermore's first big play on the New York Stock Exchange, however, the shorting of thousands upon thousands of shares of Union Pacific in a rising market promised to highball his "client"—and his partner—straight to the poor-house. Only a miracle could save them.

That miracle, appearing precisely at 5:13 A.M., on April 18, 1906, was an earthquake ripping open the innards of San Francisco. In a wink, its entire financial section—banks, brokerage houses, office buildings—all disappeared beneath the earth's crust. As if by one wave of God's hand, Stanford University and its entire campus sank into the ground. Hundreds upon hundreds of innocent humans lost their lives in the disaster. And the money-flow to and from the West Coast stopped with the suddenness of a fine watch when the mainspring snaps.

In New York City, news of the quake brought a sharp shake-out in the market. Along with other issues, Union Pacific fell like a dead duck—and Livermore promptly covered his shorts. A few days later, the "astute speculator" counted up his first killing. He paid his partner, reported the success to Thomas Lawson, and banked over $300,000.

Then he made the first of a lifelong series of errors. He bragged to the press about his killing (never mentioning the partner, of course); and Lawson heard about it in Boston. Under the code that men live by in Wall Street, Lawson naturally considered the quarter-million-plus that Livermore had pocketed really belonged to him. He bluntly demanded the profit from the "partnership account."

No need here to stretch the imagination as to what Livermore's answer was . . . He, of course, refused to part with a penny of the profits; and Lawson became his sworn stock market enemy.

Lucky Livermore couldn't have cared less. Miraculously, he had emerged as a successful speculator; now he wanted to press his bankroll into that first million.

He went about it, however, in a mighty peculiar manner. Directly after his first "killing," the elated trader decided to live it up. And why not? He was almost thirty; he was married in name only—and childless; he had developed a definite taste for luxury, and a capacity for having fun. Fun for Jesse Livermore was, simply, enjoying a beautiful woman in a comfortable bed. (And he had this kind of fun until the end of his days.)

As the spring of 1906 warmed into a blazingly hot summer, Jesse Livermore took his "fun" to Saratoga.

During the mornings he frequented the poshy boardrooms, acting artfully up to his reputation for being an important and successful man. In the afternoons, Jesse went to the races—not so much to bet, as to be seen; not so much to become known as a "sport," but as to rub elbows with people much wealthier than he—people who knew a lot more about the pools in certain stocks than did the ex-taker of bucket-shops. Dressed in the finest fashion—tweeds, high-standing Arrow collar and thin tie—Jesse Livermore reflected the picture of a

young businessman on the way up. To point up his affluence, he affected a pair of golden *pince-nez,* which he
wore suspended from his neck by an impressive black
silk ribbon.

Livermore, flushed and confident, took to eavesdrop-
ping, name-dropping and tip-dropping—and thus fell
victim to a costly error. The rule in Wall Street is, "Don't
make the same mistake once." Livermore's rule, however, was: "Don't make the same error twice." One of
Aristotle's doctrines is that learning "comes only from
suffering" . . . Livermore was certainly Aristotelian, in
thought and in practice. All his "fun" in Saratoga had
made a serious dent in his bankroll; and acting on sudden and characteristic impulse, he set out to fill that
dent.

According to the consensus of opinion at the famous
"watering-place," there was to be a forthcoming rise;
in fact, a summer rally already had run a good deal of
its customary course. Livermore logically reasoned that
the "suckers" who believed Wall Street represented a
one-way thoroughfare on the up-side had to be wrong.
Immediately, he went short. Since his first killing actually came from Union Pacific, he decided to play the
same stock. This time the pool prepared for him—and
there *was* no earthquake. Patiently they waited for Livermore to stop hitting their stock; and then they briskly
began to "wash it up" (a method of raising or lowering
a stock price by matching buy orders and sell orders at
different brokers simultaneously crossed on the Exchange floor). Today, of course, this practice is outlawed.

Seeing the price of Union Pacific jump sharply, Livermore reasoned wrongly: "If it was high enough to sell
short at $160, it should be better at $165." He sold more
short.

Now the ex-Boston board-boy became financially fractured from another—and unforeseen—source.

Suddenly, the Union Pacific Board declared a 10% stock dividend, as an "extra." And the shares zoomed. A rueful Livermore watched his more than quarter-of-a-million vanish on the up-ticks.

For the third time in thirty years, he found himself broke. This time he couldn't blame anybody else; nor was he inclined to blame himself either. He was more interested in reviewing his error. One thing became crystal-clear to the ruined trader; there appeared to be far more to the exciting game of stock market profits than either the business of accurately guessing price movements from tape-action, or the technique of charting in an attempt to forecast future movements.

In searching desperately for the reason why he had gone wrong, he soon came to realize that mere research of an issue's basic fundamentals (book value, relationship of market price to earnings, to dividends, etc.) was not enough. Even more necessary was *inside information* about management's future intentions. He also realized the truth of Daniel Drew's homey, but cogent, aphorism: "Anybody who plays the stock market not as an insider is like a man buying cows in the moonlight." Livermore solemnly vowed to himself that even if he didn't become an insider, he never would trade again without having positive information as to what they intended to do about dividends, pay-outs, etc.

However, before he could exert enough influence to extract confidential information from the usually close-mouthed directors of publicly traded companies, he had to replenish his lost bankroll. And so, forcibly swallowing his pride, he returned to New York and once again dropped in on his "ex-partner."

With another fifty-fifty deal under his belt, the wounded speculator promptly committed the entire account to a line of short sales on Great Northern. This time, his intuition (and even his most enthusiastic latter-day supporters could not attribute this maneuver to research) paid off; he effected his second killing in the market. But he was still an inconsequential factor among market greats; and he still hadn't earned his first million.

Now that Livermore was bolstered enough (financially) to resume his role of successful Wall Street speculator, what did he do? Carefully husband his funds for the next killing? Oh, no—not when it meant hanging around in a city caught in the icy grip of that 1906 winter. Jesse simply took the next sleeper and headed for the most fashionable resort in Florida; he went fishing—in Palm Beach.

The first time Livermore went out into the Gulf Stream in a chartered "yacht" to go sailfishing, he fell in love. The moment he hooked one of those fighting beauties, and successfully reeled the monster to the gaff, he himself was hooked for life. But Livermore hated to rent things. He hungered for enough money to *own* them. Then and there, he firmly decided to buy a genuine yacht.

His ambition could have been whetted by the constant inner need to prove himself as big (by reputation, at least) as the "Silver Fox"—James R. Keene. Devotees of the tape, as well as those who serve them, have been respectful always of salt-water fishermen and certainly of yachtsmen; and so Livermore busily planned his future pleasures to befit the successful personal image he was bent on building. "Nobody does business with a failure" has been a stock market dictum ever since the first trade under the Buttonwood tree on Wall Street in 1792. Livermore, time and again a financial failure, knew this better than anyone who ever traded in the

Street. He knew it from the time he earned his first dollar in a Worcester bucket-shop; and from then on, he tried frenetically to parade himself always as a huge financial success.

Livermore cut short his Palm Beach holiday in the winter of 1906-1907 to go back to Wall Street, where the market roiled six days a week and enterprising gamblers could be accommodated readily—even out on the street—by intransigent believers in the maxim: "The public is always wrong."

Luckily for Livermore, he just happened to be right.

He leaped onto the road to his first million by selling Anaconda short. Slowly, the market started to sag. This time, and wisely so, Livermore took profits on the way down. "Take some profits," he advised much later, "even if it's just to see the money. It is good to look at your money once in a while . . ."

But Livermore couldn't just sit and look at it, or hold it; it was much more fun to spend it. So, in the middle of his brilliantly-conceived plan to win money from a market decline, he took off with his current piece of "fun" for Europe. According to his pseudo-biography, he then was "a trifle more than three-quarters-of-a-million dollars to the good . . ."

Fortunately for his bankroll, he didn't linger long on the Continent. At summer's end, 1907, he returned to the market—and plunged on the short side, heavily.

With typical egotism, he later attributed the reason for his bearishness to his own brilliance in detecting a "bullish manipulation."

In retrospect, the only real money he had earned so far had been acting as a bear—always on the short side of the market. He realized with regret that losses he had suffered were due to his own stubborn refusal to admit errors before his mistakes turned into ruin. This time he conducted his bear campaign the way he was to do it in future forays—by doing balancing trades (selling short slightly more than he bought long, so as to confuse the boys on the floor; but on balance, of course, he remained short).

In the fall when the market attained a plateau, Livermore found himself in a predominantly bearish position. For days, the market meandered like a riderless horse —headed nowhere. And then rumblings of monetary restrictions pervaded the Street. Stock prices began to tumble.

Prior to the supposedly panic-free era initiated by President John Kennedy—and perpetuated by Lyndon B. Johnson—our nation systematically suffered from recurring financial revulsions. In each major money panic since the first one in 1792, the bell-wether has always been credit restriction, or "tight money." In October, 1907, such a signal burst in Wall Street with the brisance of a bomb.

Not only did money become tight, it became practically unobtainable, except at larcenous rates. Interest on call-money soared to crazy levels—100% and more, per annum. Banks immediately called in existing loans on securities; and the panic hit like a thunderbolt.

October 24, 1907, will be remembered forever as "disaster day" in Wall Street. For on that harrowing day, bids on the floor melted away, and it looked like every house in the Street would "go to the wall." Precisely on that day of financial terror, Jesse Livermore found himself a millionaire—on paper.

This also happened to be the same day on which J. P. Morgan forced his fellow capitalists to unlock their coffers and go into the market to buy.

Jesse Livermore, no matter what deserving epithets he was ever called, could hardly be classified a "financial imbecile." He noticed buying on the tape and made a few phone calls. When he found out who was sparking the rally, he covered swiftly. He knew better than to buck the Morgan crowd, and when the last order went off "at the bell" (a trade initiated when the closing gong is sounded on the floor—often the last trade in a specific issue for the day), Jesse Livermore found himself a millionaire.

The long, hard road to riches he had embarked on at the age of sixteen had taught this incurable thirty-year-old speculator a few lessons in lifemanship. But like the minister who drinks while warning his parishioners not to, Livermore wasn't sobered by his affluence. Now that his bank balance reflected seven figures (without the decimal points), he moved into a lavishly furnished apartment at 194 Riverside Drive—and he bought his yacht, the *Anita Venetian.*

In those days, Mr. George Jay Gould (Jay Gould's heir) was proudly sailing the *Atlantic,* his 300-foot, triple-screw steel yacht; and J. P. Morgan roamed the ocean in his legendary *Corsair.* The newly rich Mr. Jesse Livermore had little to be ashamed of when he registered his *Anita* with Lloyd's, and mounted the red-white-and-blue burgee of the Columbia Yacht Club on her noble bow.

The *Anita,* 202 feet over-all, was a steam-schooner of composite construction—a ship befitting the speculator's desired reputation for living like a millionaire. With the same ardor he displayed as a stock-plunger, Livermore hurled himself into the exciting role of yachtsman. Correctly attired in navy brass-buttoned bridge-coat, grey flannel trousers, and captain's hat, he thoroughly enjoyed his winter cruise to Florida.

What he enjoyed even more were rumors of his intense interest in Lillian Russell . . .

Chapter 5

COTTON KING

At that time, Lillian Russell, aptly named "The American Beauty," happened to be the inamorata of Diamond Jim Brady. She loved jewelry, of course—as did her lover, whose passion for diamonds led him to having them sewn into his pants as suspender-buttons. Diamond Jim, an ex-messenger boy for the New York Central, was then the most widely publicized millionaire in New York. His rooftop, high-kick, midnight dinners were the talk of the town.

Being linked in print with the paramour of this flamboyant tycoon, was just the kind of glamorous spice necessary to Livermore's self-waged publicity campaign on the people of New York City. How he must have puffed up with pride when the *Police Gazette* accused him of being the daring interloper who had spirited Diamond Jim's girl off to Florida by sea.

The importance of the feminine diversion which Livermore carried away to the South after his miraculous killing (a money-miracle triggered by a panic) is of little significance to the drama of his stock-trading career. What he did by way of business, however, once he got there—and "fished off the Florida coast"—is important.

The friendships he struck up in the Palm Beach office of E. F. Hutton and other board-rooms in that resort area were to affect his whole life. For it was at this time that he learned about commodities.

Livermore admitted to himself (although never to anyone else) that his first million had fallen into his hands by sheer luck; he had come to understand, only too well, the complexities influencing the course of stock market prices. Not only was value a consideration price-wise, but there was the *human* element—the people who held the big blocks; the directors, and what they intended to do about pay-outs; the pool, and how strong it was.

He soon learned that commodities, however, represented fewer problems, because their prices depended basically upon supply and demand. From conversations with friends in the Florida brokerage offices, he came to the conclusion that he should shift his efforts from the market in stocks to the purchase and sale of commodities contracts, mainly futures.

In trading commodities there are two markets: the spot market (delivery during the current month), and the futures market (delivery during a future month). There are also two kinds of traders: the hedgers and the speculators.

Hedgers are people who buy futures to protect the price of future inventory they intend to make. For example, if a baker sells bread at 15¢ a loaf, he bases this price upon a set cost for flour ground from wheat at a certain price. He wants to be sure in January that he will be able to produce 15¢ bread in July; so he buys July wheat at a price protecting his future inventory. In other words, he has hedged his business against a rise in the price of wheat during July. And, of course, he can effect a similar maneuver for other months.

Speculators in commodities, like speculators in stocks, buy and sell futures for one solitary purpose— to profit from the price changes. Oddly enough, the public has never looked upon speculators in the futures market with the disfavor they seem to arouse in the stock market. They have become sensibly accepted as a necessary force in commodities transactions in order to supply *liquidity.* Obviously, if all the bakers have already bought July wheat and farmers want to pre-sell their crop, they have to have buyers. The speculators step in to fill the void. The same, of course, is true of all commodity trading.

But Livermore learned several other things about commodity trading, even before he bought his first Wheat contract (5,000 bushels). Only a small deposit was necessary to control the price movement of a large number of bushels. Because he traded in something that wouldn't be delivered (or called for delivery) for months ahead, the remainder of the contract's value did not have to be secured; nor did the commodity purchaser have to pay interest on his debit balance at the broker's—a rate that nicked a speculator's roll when call-money soared. Finally, in consideration of the money amount controlled by the commodity speculator, the commissions just happened to be less than those charged by the Exchange members for stock transactions in similar amounts. And by now, Jesse, like any other active stock trader, had become painfully aware of the money his actions funneled into brokers' pockets.

Moreover, if a commodity speculator sold Wheat short, for example, and the price began to rise, he could stop out his liability at once by making an opposite contract. If a short-seller on the Exchange was unable to borrow shares of stock, he would be forced to go into the market to buy; and who could tell what the price would be—especially if this particular stock were in a squeeze (a small corner). This could easily cripple a trader acting as a bear. So far, this risky method of trading in the market had been the only one to throw off a profit to Livermore. So during his vacation in Palm Beach that winter, he became intensely interested in commodity price movements.

At that time, the reigning interest in the futures market happened to be Cotton. The minimum contract was for 100 bales (50,000 pounds).

In a series of quiet moves, Livermore gradually bought Cotton. He soon found himself long of 120,000 bales in a rising market for which he, himself, happened to be largely responsible. But he also was astute enough to realize that buying in any securities market is easy; selling is harder. If he represented the main buyer in Cotton, he reasoned, to whom could he sell his contracts? Of course, he knew he couldn't make any money at all from his first huge commodity play unless he sold out at a higher-than-cost figure.

To insure this, Livermore wasn't going to depend on luck . . . He would achieve it via a newspaperman.

The resultant—and planted—article (on page 1 in the New York *World*) startled the Street with its headline:

JULY COTTON CORNERED BY JESSIE LIVERMORE

The shorts swiftly covered; the suckers rushed in to buy; and Jesse Livermore unloaded.

When complimented by a fellow trader for having pulled off one of the "slickest deals ever," Livermore modestly demurred, "I had nothing to do with the article at all." With his startling success, the "Boy Plunger" earned himself a new nickname: the "Cotton King."

Livermore now hungered to belong to the "race of courtly gentlemen, whose dress, manners and temperament fit them as the plumage fits a fine bird . . ." He knew there was no place for his nagging—and ever-demanding—wife in his coveted race. But at least, his money-making worries were over. He had discovered an infallible "system" for making money in the commodities market. First, he would accumulate a huge position (long or short); second, he would influence the press to publicize his action; and finally, he would happily unload his position on the suckers. "Sell on strength" was advice which he believed had been created specifically for his own use; and, until the day he died, he never stopped believing the public was *always* wrong.

The confident, calculating, and supposedly sophisticated Cotton King, having arrived in Palm Beach with one million which he speedily parlayed into three, had some enemies. It turned out that the worst one of all was *himself*.

Instead of relaxing, or waiting for another clear-cut chance to make a killing, he assumed the role of a rich man and went looking for advice.

"Advice that costs nothing," he later said wistfully, "is worth just that." But at this point—the spring of 1908—this was something he had yet to learn.

Upon the advice of a renowned Cotton expert, Livermore found himself long of almost a half-million bales of Cotton. This time the market began to decline. Later, in the fullness of age, Livermore was to observe: "Of all the speculative blunders, there are few greater than trying to average a losing game . . ." But in the wine-cups of his youth, he tried desperately to stem the drop as he bought and bought, in New Orleans and in Liverpool until he was sold out and wiped out. When he fingered his last brokerage confirm, the one indicating the sale of his last bale of Cotton, he had been "dethroned." Not only was the Cotton King busted, but he owed a small fortune.

The *Anita* went under the hammer. The Riverside Drive apartment, with its antiques, Oriental rugs and lavish furnishings, disappeared like a cup of cold water on the hot sands of Khartoum. Livermore gave notes to his broker-creditors, and left New York for Chicago. "I'll be back," he assured them confidently, "and I'll pay you every single cent . . ."

In Wall Street, promises are only as good as their maker. In the case of Jesse Livermore, his intentions were good and his word still happened to be good; but the times were firmly against him.

Out West, he set out to again gull the bucket-shops, to scalp an existence under an assumed name, to find some trusting souls deluded enough to provide him with a trading bankroll.

The "long, lean years of 1911, 1912, 1913" dragged by agonizingly, with Livermore doing little more than remaining alive; and he went even deeper into debt to those few loyal boosters still believing in his come-back ability. By 1914, Jesse found himself living at the Bretton Hall Hotel, at 86th Street and Broadway, in New York City.

In July of that year, the New York Stock Exchange shut its doors. And until they were re-opened in December, pickings were indeed slim in the "outlaw market" conducted on the Street. Meanwhile, a bitter war raged in Europe.

"I owed more than a million dollars," Jesse later confessed to Ben Block, a broker friend, "and it looked like it was going to be a long time before I could ever make a come-back."

But there were some denizens of the paper jungle who still remembered Jesse's activities in his little hole-in-the-wall office at 35 New Street, where he had made his killing in the 1907 panic. They hungered deeply for commissions they knew Livermore could generate if he were trading.

One day in early 1915, an anonymous sage presented a harassed Livermore with a bit of fine advice: "Why don't you go bankrupt?" And he added assuringly, "This should wipe the slate clean and you can work out a new start . . ."

Never can it be said that when Livermore heard good advice he didn't react. If he decided not to use it, he simply forgot it. But if his hunches told him to *act* on it, he acted with the speed of a cobra striking. He rushed to his lawyer and filed a formal petition. As a result, he made headlines in *The New York Times* with:

COTTON KING A BANKRUPT

The article ran on to say that Livermore, "whose startling losses in Cotton . . . made him one of the well-known characters in Wall Street has filed a voluntary petition in Bankruptcy in the Federal District Court . . ."

The Livermore balance sheet reflected $102,474 in professed liabilities; and the value of his assets was unknown. He also happened to be a month behind in his rent to the hotel (now a third-class joint).

Slightly more than ninety days later, Livermore again made the *Times.* This time the headline went:

LIVERMORE'S SLATE CLEAN

Speaking of the "spectacular market speculator," the reporter said:

> Jesse Livermore, who paid brokers thousands of dollars in commissions in the time that speculation in stocks, Grain, and Copper was reported to have netted him a fortune of six million dollars, was discharged by Judge Hand from bankruptcy.

All of his indebtedness was to brokerage houses and these did not press him for payment of his debts . . .

Why?

There is only one answer. Not only did the brokers hunger for Livermore's return to the trading arena, but a good portion of the notes representing Livermore's debts arose when he received a split of the commissions, and the Exchange firms took back notes for protection (in case the Exchange should accuse the houses of having greased-off Livermore in order to keep him alive).

In any event, the pattern became set. It was one Livermore depended upon time and again in extricating himself from financial difficulty.

Livermore—uneducated except in the world of hard knocks around board-rooms—developed an amazingly simple philosophy about people. He classified them broadly into three groups:

1. Those who learn by knowledge.
2. Those who learn by experience.
3. Those who never learn at all.

Only slightly chastened by his first lesson in bankruptcy, Livermore had little time for philosophy or learning. Obsessed with his *idée fixe* that the market owed him a living, he had to win his bankroll back—and beat the market at the same time.

But now he had to change his tactics. No longer could he hope to trade at a brokerage firm for his own account. He was forced now to fall back on that old ruse, the partnership discretionary account.

It would seem that securing the suckers' consent to having their funds managed by a bankrupt would present some difficulties; but it turned out to be easier than he had thought. Livermore, who considered Wall Street to be a "giant whorehouse" where partners were "madams," the customers' men, "pimps," and stocks "whores" the customers threw their money away on, was readily accommodated. With the aid of some good-natured "madam," Livermore—a regular loser with his own money—became saddled with the responsibility of earning profits for strangers.

Chapter 6

THE BIG LEAK

Livermore applied himself diligently to the handling of other people's money; he struck up friendships with ambitious brokers like Bernard Baruch (then, of course, called "Barney"); and so, slowly, he managed to acquire his own trading bankroll. Admittedly, he didn't amount to much. As a factor influencing the direction of stock prices, Jesse, compared to a giant such as Thomas Fortune Ryan, was then a mere pipsqueak. But because of his perennial ability to ingratiate himself with people who counted, Livermore became quite friendly with the important brokers (J. R. Williston, E. F. Hutton, et al.).

He also began to call upon a small army of "bird dogs" (steerers of accounts to brokers), "pointers" (touts hired to drop tips for market manipulators), and saleable financial writers to provide him with private information—for which he readily paid, either with his own or his clients' money. He further arranged for a definite split of the Stock Exchange commissions he generated—which, of course, even then represented an illegal practice for Exchange members.

But the brokers were hungry, and they willingly paid Livermore for business he brought them, just as though he was acting as a customer's man. And he, in turn, handed the brokers farcical notes.

Livermore's station in Wall Street deteriorated quickly to that of a stock market prostitute. Still, he burned with secret ambition, and strode silently and proudly through the financial district. "Someday," he kept saying to himself, "I'm going to be just like Bet-A-Million Gates. I'll have—just like him—a 'blind following.' And what the papers will say I did in the market will make the public do the same. This way I'll really get rich . . ."

Stalling his many creditors, and unmindful of the war raging across the ocean (he didn't care whether America entered the conflict or stayed out), Jesse Livermore took his secret hopes—and the train—down to Palm Beach, as winter of 1916-1917 first kissed New York's sidewalks with snowflakes.

During his brief but enjoyable seasons as yachtsman, Jesse had cemented firm friendships with T. Coleman Du Pont, the Lewisohn Brothers, and several other well-heeled citizens. Also, he maintained small trading accounts at both E. F. Hutton and Block, Maloney. What little commodity trading he then dabbled in was gingerly carried on the books of J. R. Williston. To avoid showing his hand, Jesse often did an active give-up business at other brokers.

In this type of transaction, orders are placed and executed at firms where the actual buyer or seller does not maintain an account. The accommodating broker enters and fills the stranger's orders, and gives them up for clearance to that visitor's regular brokerage house; and the Exchange commission is split on a fifty-fifty basis (legal, of course). It was an invariable practice by market manipulators to "give up" orders to firms for two purposes: one, to generate commissions in houses in which promoters didn't maintain accounts, but whose production personnel might become valuable friends; and two, to hide their hands in transactions they might wish to conceal from fellows on the Exchange floor.

On the morning of December 20, 1916, Jesse Livermore attentively watched the boards in the Palm Beach office of Finlay, Barrel & Company—even though he did not maintain an account there. Suddenly, he became alerted to a telegram wired from Finlay's home office in Chicago. This happened to be a flash wire predicated upon information dispatched by a mendacious Washington reporter named W. W. Price.

In effect, the wire revealed that later in the day, President Wilson would ask the warring parties to end hostilities and bring back peace to a troubled world.

Livermore knew this move was bound to lead to a market collapse. Knowing that if the President sent such a wire, stocks "would fall out of bed," Jesse wasted no time thinking. He acted.

Back in Boston, meanwhile, his old benefactor, Thomas W. Lawson, happened to be long thousands of shares of stock in a bullish attempt at a market come-back. Whether Livermore knew this or not is debatable; but he did know in advance about the President's proposed telegram, and on that he had to get going . . .

Swiftly he fired give-up orders through every broker he could contact by phone or wire. Naturally, he let his own clique of New York brokers in on the news—after he had successfully let out a huge line of shorts on leading, and normally strongly sponsored, issues like the "Four Horsemen" (Steel, American Can, Baldwin, and Anaconda).

At 1:45 P.M., W. G. Toomey, chief of E. F. Hutton's telegraph department, circulated a flash wire to all branches—leaking the news of President Wilson's peace note hours before the actual event.

At once, the market began to sag. And when news of the peace note actually hit the floor of the Exchange, there was utter chaos. Bids melted away; and prices dropped swiftly like lead-sinkers in a fresh-water lake.

Boston Lawson lost everything he had in the world, except his "good" name. Blaming his financial destruction on the market operation of Messrs. Baruch and Livermore, this "lamb" bleated loudly—and long. He came up with quite a few stunning accusations: first, that the President's brother-in-law happened to be a partner in the Washington, D.C., office of F. A. Connolly & Company, brokers, who were aware of Mr. Wilson's note hours before its public announcement. Lawson went on to claim that because firms like Hutton had leaked "secret" information, they had helped their customers coin fortunes at the expense of the rest of the country. Finally, he stormed, manipulators like Barney Baruch and Jesse Livermore should be seized immediately, locked up in an escape-proof jail—with the key hurled into the nearest ocean.

Lawson's charges brought Congressional action. A select committee promptly began to dig into the "leak." Baruch candidly admitted having made a mere $465,000, as the result of his advance knowledge of the President's dove-like overture. Livermore, however, told the committee nothing. In fact, he complained, he had acted as an innocent party who always sold stocks short when they appeared over-priced. And he attributed his leak-note clean-up to an innocent accident—his happening to notice the premature telegram in a strange broker's office.

As a result of the investigation, the New York Stock Exchange amended its rules, and forbade its members forever after to act on "leak tips."

This did not apply, of course, to Livermore; for he did not belong to "the club." He was an outside speculator, whose prime consideration was always himself; and to himself he chuckled indeed, at the noise the committee made in the press. He could not resist a happy smile, as he asked his banker what his balance happened to be—after the bills had been paid inadvertently by his country's President.

In speaking of Livermore's activities at this time, Sherman Whipple insisted that the Stock Exchange eliminate both short selling and margin trading. It's interesting to conjecture as to what might have happened had the Exchange listened to Mr. Whipple . . . But Jesse Livermore paid little heed to carping critics. Once again, he had a trading bankroll—with enough left over to fulfill some grandiose plans for the future.

Learning by default is generally a painful process; but often it is the one best remembered. Livermore had learned enough in his suffering during the lean years to now make up for something he had neglected to do at the time he had money. He determined to provide himself with a permanent "meal-ticket."

This buffer against bad times started out as a half-million-dollar annuity, slanted to throw off a return of about $30,000 a year to its owner. And it looked as though its owner, Jesse Livermore, at last would have something substantial to fall back on if he again went wrong in the market. "Provide yourself with a meal-ticket first," he later advised, "then even if you are wrong about the market, at least you can still eat."

Typically, now—and in keeping with his profligate tastes—Livermore also rushed right out and bought a huge speedboat, which he called a "sub-catcher." He did this primarily to attract the attention of the papers. He also bought a platinum-and-emerald ring for $120,-000.

The boat (or rather, ship) he considered to be a necessary prop for a stock market millionaire. But who was to be the lucky recipient of the emerald solitaire?

Police Gazette, amazingly accurate about Livermore's

escapades, hinted broadly that there would be a new, a second Mrs. Jesse Livermore soon (once he rid himself of the old, the first Mrs. Livermore legally called his "wife").

This proved to be difficult—and annoying. Eventually, four-fifths of the Livermore meal-ticket ($400,000) passed over in trust to nettlesome Nettie. Not satisfied with mere money, this militant marriage "partner" asserted her rights and made off with all the antiques and the furniture—including Jesse's beloved Rolls.

Although Livermore didn't mind losing a good part of his hard-times buffer, or his valuable goodies and chattels, he deeply resented relinquishing his Rolls into the grasping hands of a female he had long since come to hate. So he sent the famous ex-District Attorney, W. Travers Jerome, to Huntington, Long Island, to replevin the car.

Mr. Jerome could hardly be described as a retiring individual. His fabled pursuit—the capture and subsequent conviction of Pittsburgh millionaire Harry Thaw, who in 1906 had murdered the renowned architect Stanford White—gave the lawman an international reputation for performance. So with speed and aplomb—and a second set of keys—W. Travers Jerome, his handle-bar moustaches bristling in the sun, plopped himself behind the wheel of the magnificent machine parked at Mrs. Livermore's country place) and headed it down the road toward the city.

But Nettie refused to be intimidated. Speedily she summoned state troopers, who not only pulled the Rolls over (before it had rolled very far) but also slapped W. Travers Jerome into the local calaboose—charged with stealing the car.

Jerome, of course, quickly got himself "sprung"; and Mrs. Livermore readily withdrew the charges. The resultant publicity proved to be just fine for Livermore—and for his future. Newsmen, hungry for something spicy, jumped at juicy tidbits Livermore offered: his marital troubles, revelation as to who his lawyer was and exaggerated details of his stock market coup (one source said he had made "$10,000,000 in thirty minutes").

He readily obliged members of the working press. So charmed were they with the polished, beleaguered, speculator that they publicized him as a "new breed of trader." And how pleased Jesse must have been to sit down to a Sunday breakfast and savor a special feature article in the *Times* on the two knowing traders, Bernard Baruch and Jesse Livermore, who recently had capitalized upon the "leak."

Touching upon the operations of this devious pair, the *Times* writer gushed:

> ... The speculator in stocks of the present day is more of a student and economist than the sensational manipulator of other years ...

The deluded reporter then ran on to say that Livermore and Baruch did not indulge in "self-advertising and loud boasting in the lobbies of up-town hotels ..."

(In his memoirs, Baruch admits to having made a pile by selling a certain Copper stock short just before he entered a huge liquidating order for one of his clients, T. F. Ryan—an unpardonable thing for any broker to do.)

Speaking specifically of Livermore's shrewdness and courage, the *Times* man said, "He sensed the market tendency and stood unmoved amid a shower of optimistic utterances ..."

How Livermore laughed with relish as he devoured each word! For each word was a building-block in the construction of the *phoniest* legend ever built and foisted upon devotees of the stock market game.

Armed now with an international reputation as a successful stock market operator worth millions ("If I only had Livermore's money" became part of the language of the times)—and bolstered enough financially to pay the expenses of a new life (that would include a new wife)—Jesse promptly unloaded his old marriage partner, via the Reno route, in October 1917.

On the evening of December 2, 1918, in a simple ceremony at the St. Regis Hotel, the affluent speculator and his latest love were married. With Magistrate Peter B. Barlow officiating, Jesse slipped a wedding ring onto the hand of his bride. Engraved inside the ring was this fervent dedication: "Dotsie for ever and ever. JL."

The second Mrs. Livermore (alive at the time of this writing) happened to be the daughter of a rich, retired, Brooklyn merchant named Wendt. A bride for the first time, Dorothy Wendt Livermore could hardly repress her excitement. After all, she was an innocent eighteen—and her handsome husband, a virile forty-one.

Inspired by his new wife's love, a new life opened for Jesse Lauriston Livermore. At last—and for the first time —he tried to become legitimate; he wanted to be respectable. He almost succeeded.

PART II

THE LIVERMORE LIFE

*". . . I haven't been called Jesse for
years. Everybody, my family included,
calls me: J.L. . . ."*

> *The New York Times*
> May 23, 1927, p. 23.

Chapter 7

EVERMORE

The day after Jesse Livermore married the "love of his life" he carried her proudly over the threshold of a sumptuously furnished town-house at 8 West 76th Street, in New York City. Reviving his dream of being accepted by one and all as a rich gentleman, he settled down seriously to win the things he hadn't had time for: a family, a professional status in the brokerage community, club memberships, etc. But what he hungered for most was simply the admiration and respect of the "suckers."

In 1918, the *Times* observed that the era of the "swash-buckling trader had ended;" and it assured its readership that the new kind of speculator made his market moves intelligently, after weighing the facts. But the *Times* erred badly in its assessment of Livermore ... At that time, he was consumed with a desire for the kind of recognition that swashbuckling Jim Fisk had had. This desire was greater than any other he could think of, including having fun with his new wife. But Jesse, gifted with the cunning of an alley-cat, didn't dispute the newspaper distortions of his true motives. Instead, he changed his *modus operandi.*

Believing that the market owed him a living, he had attempted heretofore to get rich from trading profits. Now he realized that profits could come easier if he became an integral part of the brokerage community, and managed some "blind pools" himself. And so he became a legitimate broker. On January 2, 1920, Jesse Livermore purchased a seat on the New York Curb for $5,000. Now he was privileged to stand out in the Street and trade.

Jesse's big money, however, didn't come from the trades he conducted out on the "curb." In fact, there is little evidence to indicate that he ever appeared on the Street to actively partake in the excitement and action of a busy session. Instead, he concentrated on profits from pool operations.

Meanwhile, in 1919, his obliging wife presented him with an heir: Jesse L. Livermore, Jr.

The thought of raising his scion in the hot city was anathema to the high-living broker; so he bought an estate: Locust Lawn, in Sands Point, Great Neck, New York.

During the summer now, the Livermores sojourned on the cool shores of Long Island Sound. The grounds of Locust Lawn—thirteen beautifully landscaped acres—rolled regally down to the water's edge. The estate-house itself, more than a century old, was a farmer's dream-house; but the new Mrs. Livermore soon made some radical changes.

While her husband hustled away at his office in the City (at 111 Broadway), the energetic bride busied herself with plans to renovate, to enlarge, and to beautify her home. Eventually, the farm-house underwent a magical change. It turned into a great manor "two stories high, 29 rooms, 12 baths, and a basement containing a bar, a play-room and a completely appointed barbershop."

Obviously, the new plumbing came first. And in 1923—even before the estate-house had been renovated—Mrs. Livermore handed her admiring husband another son: Paul Alexander.

Naturally, the young wife—so loved, and so loving—dreamed this wonderful way of life would last forever. Hopefully, she renamed the estate: EVERMORE.

For some years, the Livermores' idyll remained blissful and unsullied. From youth on, Jesse displayed the morals of a jack-rabbit; but now he controlled himself diligently looking after the business of earning enough to pay for the high cost of living which he had established for his family. Flaunting his wide-spread reputation of being able to "move a stock up or down at will," Livermore found avid sponsors ready to pay for his talents.

Of course, his reputation as a talented leader of pools in then-legal market manipulations was swiftly bruited about by well-paid underlings, hired to create and maintain an aura of greatness around their leader. And they did their job well: Livermore got his first big "legal" chance in the fall of 1921. It came in letter-form—a pool-agreement deal with the powerful Lewisohn Brothers that went something like this:

> . . . Confirming the agreement of this morning whereby you are to have the management of a pool formed to operate in Seneca Copper, you have the power to buy and sell shares of the subject stock at your discretion.
>
> If the pool account is cancelled, and the pool is long stock, the debit will be distributed as follows. If profits have accrued to the pool when its operation is ended, a like distribution will be made . . .
>
> Kindly signify your acceptance in writing on the copy of this letter appended . . .
>
> Walter Lewisohn

Seneca Copper, a vehicle of the Lewisohns, had come

out as an over-the-counter issue at $12. Shortly after the pool was formed, Livermore began to take the stock up; and four months later, the issue traded at the $25-level. Suddenly—and with no explanation—the Lewisohns abruptly cancelled his powers. Why? . . . Did they fear their trusted pool-manager might have visions of raiding their stock? This question never was answered; for thereafter, Livermore stayed away from Seneca as if it had syphilis.

*   *   *   *   *

In the summer of 1922, Jesse Livermore was reputed to have lost $8,500,000 for himself—and for his associates—because, foolishly, he had been on the "short side of the market in Mexican Pete." Moreover, it was alleged that when Livermore found himself badly squeezed by the bulls, he resorted to a stock market coward's stratagem: reputedly, he made a "private settlement" (ended his abortive market position by negotiation off the floor of the Exchange). The anonymous perpetrators of this story, to give it even more spice, added the rumor that Livermore—in the midst of his struggle—found time enough to attend an old flame's funeral.

In rebuttal, Livermore bitterly protested:

> . . . The day I was supposed to attend Lillian Russell's funeral services, I was in my office until 5 P.M. . . . The day I was supposed to have settled with the Mexican Pete people, I was at Poughkeepsie watching the boat races . . . I have never made a private settlement in my life, nor will I.

But the knowing ones who haunted the Street knew it was standard operating procedure for stock market operators never to tell newsmen the truth unless they had to; and in this regard, Jesse Livermore was no more an exception than was the legendary "Uncle Russell" (Sage).

* * * * *

In June of 1922, the New York Stock Exchange listed for trading the shares of a grocery-chain called Piggly-Wiggly Stores. The get-up-and-go genius behind this food-retailing giant was Clarence Saunders, a fat, forty-ish man from Memphis (Tennessee).

Shortly after Piggly-Wiggly had been listed, the dynamic Mr. Saunders watched worriedly as the price of his shares declined. He quickly realized that to keep his shares trading at a fair price, he needed professional help. So he rounded up a "loan of ten million dollars, stuffed in a suitcase"*—and stormed up to New York to lick the boys on the floor.

The blustering Mr. Saunders hired a proper hunter to "kill the bears" . . . His canny choice was supposedly the greatest bear of all: Jesse Lauriston Livermore.

In November, 1922, with Livermore as his "chief of staff," Saunders initiated "the last corner in Stock Exchange history." At the time Livermore began his play, there were only 200,000 shares of Piggly-Wiggly issued and outstanding. By the end of his first week of inconspicuous buying, Livermore had gathered together 105,-000 shares in the open market; and he had barely disturbed the going price of $35 for the shares. But by March, 1923, Livermore's assiduous buying-up of shares had moved the price to over $70.

In the process, not only had he moved the market to more than double its level (from the time he began his foray against the bears), but he had also accumulated

---

*See: *Annals of Finance,* by John Brooks, *The New Yorker,* June 6, 1959, pp. 128 ff.

for Saunders 198,872 out of the 200,000 shares held by the public. In doing so, Livermore—as well as Saunders —realized that the shorts would be annihilated if Saunders suddenly demanded *delivery.*

And he suddenly did. On March 19th he asked Livermore to "spring the trap" on the shorts. The demand was accompanied by a gracious offer to be kind when asked for a "private settlement." Livermore was now faced with the most difficult decision of his entire Wall Street career. If he obeyed Saunders, the noble soul would squeeze millions from the very people Livermore depended upon for his daily bread. Of course, Livermore—acting as an agent on a percentage basis—would reap a like, but smaller fortune himself. But too many people he knew would be broken in the process. So, with the decisiveness of a soldier committing himself to a deadly mission, Livermore reneged. He resigned as chief of Saunders' operations, and left the Tennessee tycoon to carry on by himself.

The following day, Saunders himself closed the trap. From an opening trade of 75½, the stock skyrocketed to $124! In the early afternoon a rumor pervaded the floor that the Exchange just might suspend trading in the issue because Saunders had "cornered the stock." The price plummeted to $82—and rumor became truth.

After the close of that historic session, the Board of Governors of the Exchange suspended trading in shares of Piggly-Wiggly Stores. Livermore's broker friends were saved.

Saunders eventually went broke; but to his dying day, he blamed the failure of his corner on Livermore.

*   *   *   *   *

The most headache-producing pool operation that Livermore ever had turned out to be the one he rigged in Mammoth Oil.

The fall of 1922 found Jesse Livermore operating from an office at 111 Broadway, where more than fifty direct wires from brokerage houses funneled into his sanctum. At that time, he succeeded in forming a selling group to market 151,000 shares of Mammoth Oil at $40 a share. Mammoth happened to be the Sinclair Oil Company subsidiary which had managed to obtain lucrative oil leases from the U.S. Navy, through the intervention of the then-Secretary of the Interior, Albert Fall.

After the issue had gone public (Livermore in later testimony bragged that it had been "overwhelmingly subscribed"), broker Livermore had been charged by the sponsors with maintaining an orderly market in the issue. To insure this condition, he needed ready buyers. As always, this to-be-hoped-for condition readily could be aroused by inciting the greed of the investing public —in print, that is.

And so Livermore began a steady release of bullish, highly colored—and indeed highly optimistic—statements to the press. On November 1, 1923, the obliging *Times* reported:

"Bears Take A Drubbing. Jesse Livermore who led them six months ago joins ranks of the bulls . . . Six months ago he advised the public stock prices were in for a decline."

And the dedicated *Times* man then added, "His forecast proved correct."

Livermore, now heralded as a market spokesman, readily declared, "Stocks of the better-managed and conservatively capitalized corporations should be bought for substantial profits . . ." Such advice is, of course, timeless—as timeless as any issued by any market sage. And Livermore didn't confine his comments to the stock market alone: "The European war is over and the people of those countries are back planting their normal wheat acreage . . ." (He happened to be short of May Wheat and was trying, surreptitiously, to break commodity prices).

As far as *Rails* were concerned, the market mouthpiece predicted a "record Year" with a "big part of the three billion lost by investors in the past fifteen years" to be recovered soon. Naturally, Livermore's secret hope was that "suckers" would gobble up Rail shares so he could go short some more—at a healthy, high price.

Indeed, this perennial bear now cried out against those "calamity howlers" (political and statistical) who warned that the nation seemed to be heading for an economic bust. Mr. Livermore became so popular that a "testimonial dinner was tendered to him" (who gave the dinner was never determined); and he became so patriotic, so filled with love for his native land, that he contributed $2,500 to the Harding fund. (T. F. Ryan gave $5,000.)

In the midst of Livermore's stock market soothsayings, the Teapot Dome scandal erupted like a festering carbuncle—spraying odium upon everyone ever connected with it. The search for Livermore as operator of the Mammoth pool, was on . . . His expert testimony was needed. For months, he artfully managed to avoid the subpoena-server. When, finally, he was served and made his appearance, Livermore's behavior was that of any honest and outraged citizen . . . "My home address is plainly listed in the City Directory," he stormed, "and any bank or brokerage house in the United States could tell the Marshal where to find me . . ."

When Samuel Untermyer, that staunch upholder of bench and bar, learned Livermore had been summoned before the oil-lease investigators, he said acidly:

> "As this gentleman is not in the business of manipulating stock markets for his health it is

to be hoped the committee will give him a little
attention . . ."

The committee gave him a *lot* of attention—but
learned little. Slick as the oil he was supposed to talk
about, Livermore told them that all he got for floating
Mammoth, and then maintaining the issue in the market,
was a mere $9,916. Incredibly enough, the inquisitors
believed him, and let him go. His associates, however—
oilmen E. L. Doheny and Harry F. Sinclair—were indicted
for bribery. Sinclair was later sentenced to nine months
in prison, with a fine of $1,000 for contempt. Doheny,
miraculously, got off scot-free.

On December 28, 1923, Jesse Livermore left with his
family for Palm Beach, and a three-months' stay at the
Breakers. Included in his menage was his own telegraph
operator, who would be busily employed working a private wire to New York.

One of the first messages he fired off to the papers
involved, of course, the Teapot Dome scandal, in which
the first American Cabinet officer in history was sent to
jail for dereliction of duty.

In connection with the guilt of Secretary of the Interior
Fall, Livermore assured the *Times* that "men of higher
calibre should be sent to Washington." And he continued, "This country is a business nation; and it should
have at the head of its various governmental branches
the most successful businessmen in the country."

Was Livermore looking for an appointed, or elected
office? Definitely not. His comments were an integral
part of his steady scheme to assure the success of his
all-absorbing interest—making a living from changing
prices.

*   *   *   *   *

Of course, there was a myriad of other pools and market manipulations. In the fall of 1924, the world of Wall Street raged with a severe epidemic of "Radio fever." At the height of this mania, Livermore floated his last public issue as a broker: 75,000 shares of DeForest Radio— over-subscribed at $24 a share. This "hot issue" (which later went bankrupt) enjoyed an eager reception from the investing public and brokers alike; and Livermore garnered enough wherewithal to enjoy another expensive season at the Palm Beach Breakers.

The knowing ones in Wall Street had long considered Livermore to be a master at surreptitiously influencing the members of the Fourth Estate; so it was not surprising when he was suddenly catapulted into the limelight again by newspaper stories that he was using his Palm Beach base to fire wires and influence the nation's press. At this, Livermore righteously blustered: "There will be no more personal messages sent or given by me to anyone . . ." And with this, the "injured" manipulator took his wounded ego and ran out to the Gulf Stream in his new yacht, the *Gadfly*.

Now, his own personal flag fluttered boldly on the bow of his ship. It was a Prussian blue pennant flaunting a huge white letter "C" superimposed over an "O." The flag, of course, signified its owner was still the Cotton King.

Under the burning sun of the Caribbean, Jesse hooked a giant amberjack (probably a tuna) and started a long, hard struggle with the fighting fish. After battling the monster for fifty-five minutes, Jesse suddenly let go of the rod and fainted in his fishing-chair.

The captain carried him to his bunk; and he stayed out of the sun for two days. Upon the ship's return to port, he was recovered enough to wire the Times that his party had hauled in 256 fish, including a giant "whip-ray harpooned in the Gulf Stream, weighing 500 pounds and measuring 30 feet by 22 feet"—not counting the stinging tail.

These were indeed halcyon times for Jesse Lauriston Livermore. Madly in love with his wife and his sons—who adored him—the "Boy Plunger" had come a long way since the day he ran away from his father's plow-horse. In the market, and in the minds of devotees of the nation's financial pages, Livermore's name had become synonymous with wisdom and sagacity, shrewdness, boldness, and stock market success. He had become a man to be respected, to be admired and feared—but most of all, a man to be followed.

With fame, however, came the inevitable threats and nuisances . . . Livermore was menaced by mobsters seeking to kidnap his sons and hold them for ransom. He was besieged by begging letters—especially from traders who had gone broke following his advice. Yet so admired was he that one enthusiast, a seventy-year-old kitchen-worker in Paterson, New Jersey, inundated him with tips based upon the *Book of Revelations*. When the ungrateful speculator set the police on this well-meaning soul, the poor man explained he had only sent the tips as "acts of kindness to prevent Livermore from making market mistakes."

The kindly-intentioned tips came rather late in the day. Once again, Livermore began to hurl himself recklessly toward the rocks of ruin. This time, he made the fatal error of trying to break a bullish speculator—a much better market strategist than Livermore could ever hope to be. And he compounded the error by not waiting to meet his bullish adversary in a familiar arena—Wall Street. Livermore's regrettable choice of battle-field was the Chicago Wheat pit. And the man he set out to break just happened to be one of the greatest traders in stock market history. His name—little remembered to-day—was Arthur Cutten.

Chapter 8

CUTTEN

Arthur Cutten was born in Guelph, Ontario, in 1870—seven years before the birth of his market enemy, Jesse Livermore. Like Jesse, young Cutten labored on a farm; and he, too, distracted himself with pleasant fantasies of possessing untold riches when he grew to manhood.

But Cutten turned out to be a different kind of dreamer than his counterpart, Livermore. No precipitate plunger was he; rather, he was like the farmer who sits on the fence in the morning and looks at the field for several hours before mounting his tractor; and when asked why he sits so long before commencing the plowing, he answers, "I was planning. Half the plowing is in the planning . . ." So the ambitious farmboy seriously and carefully laid his money-making plans.

In 1890, Arthur Cutten—aged twenty, of medium height, slim, strong and bronzed from steady toil under the Canadian sun—journeyed to Chicago to win his fortune. He had with him the sum of fifty dollars carefully husbanded during the past five years. He soon landed a clerical job at A. S. White & Company, commodity brokers—at a salary of four dollars a week.

In true Horatio Alger style, this hard-working clerk stuck assiduously to his menial task—exercising always the kind of frugal prudence for which Dr. Franklin has been so well remembered. "Save one penny more each day than you spend" became and remained a banner for Arthur Cutten to the day of his demise. It is quite understandable, then, that as his employers repaid his diligence with regular raises, Cutten managed to save up the enormous sum of one thousand dollars—a Herculean task taking all of five years.

When the modest, self-effacing, young man of twenty-five realized he had a bankroll of a thousand dollars, he daringly decided to risk it all in the Wheat pit. His decision came only after long, long years of study of the operations of the commodity exchanges. Why hadn't he risked his small capital before? Cutten's answer was "Why should I risk my money before I know what I am doing?" Towards the end of 1895, Cutton decided he not only "knew" what he was doing, but the time to do it appeared highly propitious.

He promptly approached his employer, Mr. White, and asked for permission to open a Grain-trading account with the firm. Surprised that such a steady citizen should suddenly express a desire to gamble in the Grain pits, Mr. White advised his employee that the best thing for any "man of small means" was to always avoid the market in any way, shape, manner or form.

But this young man, who had carefully prepared for this day with years of learning in the "shadows of the Pigeon Roost that hovers over the pit," could not be dissuaded. Confident in his long-suppressed trading ability, Cutten opened an account with another firm (without telling White, of course) and plunged into the maelstrom of the Wheat pit with his hard-earned thousand.

Three months later, he quietly entered Mr. White's office. Coolly dropping his alpaca coat onto his employer's desk, Cutten told his boss, in a carefully modulated, respectful tone, that he had just been elected to membership in the Chicago Board of Trade. How had this come about?

Using the "silence, courage and pertinacity" with which he later climbed to the top of the trading-heap in Wall Street, Cutten had reaped a small fortune—and had bought a seat. He never worked for anybody again till the end of his days.

In the meantime, he attracted a small, select group of people who rightfully trusted his ability to trade for them. He soon acquired a loyal following.

Back in 1902, a legendary trader in commodities named James A. Patten had startled the speculating world with a swift, two-million-dollar profit in Wheat. In so doing, he had squeezed the price of Wheat from $1 a bushel to $1.34. This "Patten Corner" aroused the attention of Federal authorities, and for the first time ever, they tried to effect restraints upon commodity traders.

In 1924, Cutten, an incurable bull, forced the price of Wheat over the $2-a-bushel-level for the first time in history; and with that, he easily inherited Patten's mantle of fame.

Now Cutten, like Livermore, became *news*. His feats, his exploits in the Grain pit were luridly aired in every major paper in the country. In Chicago, people murmured his name with awe; and it was echoed by his devoted following. Because of this, the speculative fever swept Chicago, and the pits roared as "two-dollar Wheat" brought out the "new kings."

"Everybody seems to be making a profit," the headlines blared . . . Mrs. Scott Durand, a Chicago society luminary, became featured as the first "Queen of the Pit" . . . In a single week, Evelyn Comstock, an advertising executive, made $20,000 on a $1,000 risk . . . With call options on Grain contracts costing as little as $12.50 per call, taxi-drivers pooled their tips to get some bets down . . . One shrewd entrepreneur opened a "School for Scientific Speculation," charging $100 for a two-week course, with money-back guaranteed if the students didn't get a chance to make money during the course.

And so it went. Chicago became a crazy-mad commodity world, with Cutten as the chief spokesman and "high priest." Invariably, he was asked, "How will Wheat go?" "Higher," was his curt and perennial answer. No sooner were his comments printed than people rushed in and bought—and the market zoomed higher!

But who did the selling?

The answer seemed to be foreordained: Jesse L. Livermore, mainly.

In 1924, the "Great Bear" Jesse—attracted by the sensational news of this new Wheat king—jaundicedly eyed the skyward course of Wheat, Corn and Rye prices. "Gravity works in the market as well as in science," he believed. He was firmly convinced that what goes up must come down. Understandably, Livermore now acted according to his pattern. On the strength of one of his hunches, and without one anxious thought, he started to hit the Grain market short—a market in which Cutten and his dedicated crowd were buying.

Why Livermore didn't pull in his horns before he suffered serious financial injury is one of those market mysteries whose solution might lie in Livermore's theory of waiting for the big "swing." "The only time I ever made big money," he later confessed, "was when I sat tight and kept my position."

If this were the strategy he now employed, it led to disaster.

By the end of 1925, Livermore had lost more than three million dollars (most to Cutten), and he found himself out of commodity money. It was at this point that he gave the lie-direct to his eternal boast. "I never quit." He did, in fact, quit.

Cutten, however, happened to be some five million dollars to the good. When asked about the secret of his success, he answered abruptly, "Nerve. It takes nerve to speculate in the market . . ." Referring to ruined traders like Livermore, he added contemptuously, "Brokers . . . Hmph! Most of them are that, the broke part." And then designating Livermore in particular, he asserted, "They know the game in and out; they trade for other people, but they can't trade for themselves . . ."

Having accomplished such a stunning victory over the man reputed to be the most dangerous snake-in-the-Wall-Street-grass since Jay Gould, Cutten confidently shifted his trading attention to an unfamiliar area.

He abandoned, temporarily, his 800-acre farm in DuPage County, Illinois, with its great rambling house, 20 work horses, 80 cows, and 500 hogs—and took his wife (they had no children) to New York. There, he set up a new base of operations in a modest town-house in midtown, just off Fifth Avenue.

As soon as the Cuttens were settled, the head of the family carried his money-bags down to Wall Street to search for bargains.

One stunning trading success followed the other. Cutten cleaned up more than ten million dollars in Baldwin Locomotive—and more than eighteen millions in Montgomery Ward; and he made a multi-million-dollar killing when he moved Radio up from $40 to $450 in less than a year! By December of 1928, Arthur Cutten exerted the greatest single trading influence on Wall Street since the days of Russell Sage. Since 1926, he had been filing the largest income-tax return of any individual using the Chicago area as a home address—including the Field heirs. And so famous had he become that *The New York Times* devoted a full-page feature article to him, with the banner headline:

CUTTEN CRACKS WHIP OVER THE STOCK MARKET

In the dog-eat-dog world that happens to be Wall Street, when someone makes money, somebody else usually loses. In Cutten's clean-up, who were the losers? And how did the supposedly shrewd Mr. Livermore fare after his abortive attempt to break the cold, careful, meticulous operator that Arthur Cutten proved to be?

Livermore was not only hurt in the market; but, on April 10, 1925—having practically been driven to drink on reading of Cutten's repeated successes—he stepped out into a dark stairway at *Evermore* and fell down a flight of unfinished stairs. With his right arm so conveniently broken, he could hardly write checks . . . And when Livermore was reported to have sold 50,000,000 bushels of Wheat short, Samuel Untermyer snorted, "Fifteen million is more likely . . ."

During the summer of 1925, the feeble flicker of Livermore's attempt to recapture public interest was reflected in the *Times*, with:

> Livermore trading again . . . He conducts stock
> operations from Lake Placid . . . and is sup-
> posed to have bought 50,000 shares of Steel
> and White Motors . . .

True, Livermore was at his lodge in the Adirondacks, but he hadn't gone there to relax—or to trade at arm's length from the treacherous marketplace. Actually, he had gone there to sell the property, because he had been caught in a frightening squeeze by his creditors. The *Gadfly*, of course, went under the hammer. And the following May, Mr. Livermore disposed of his curb seat. His days as a New York broker came to a quiet end.

Yet, so cannily did he manage the leakage of publicity about his financial straits that on May 14, 1926, the *Times* revealed:

>Jesse L. Livermore . . . plans to take a trip
>around the world in his new $1,000,000 motor-
>yacht. Within the past two years he has paid
>little attention to the stock market, confining
>his operations to Wheat and to Cotton.

But it was neither Wheat nor Cotton that saved him at this time from another bankruptcy. In the spring of 1927, a pool was clandestinely formed, to be managed—secretly—by Livermore. It was, of course, a *bullish pool*, and Jesse now made the biggest killing in his life on the long side. When the news hit the street, Livermore again found himself basking in the radiance of the headlines:

LIVERMORE IN $4 MILLION COUP WALL STREET
HEARS . . .

But how did they hear? The answer is obvious. Livermore purposely leaked the news to *The New York Times*. By his own testimony, he claimed to have made this huge killing in a market play (which he managed) in Freeport Texas stock. Taking the issue quietly under control, Livermore had cleverly maneuvered the price from $19 to $74½—where he blew off his bundle. This manipulation had taken more than a year to accomplish; but when the ex-Cotton King bowed out of Freeport Texas, he had won enough to pay off all his bankruptcy claims—and a "passel" of bills besides.

Although, overtly, he seemed finished in the market, the fact is, for many years, Jesse Livermore had found a steady source of funds elsewhere: mainly, in real estate —the Florida kind. In 1908, when the ambitious speculator first sailed into West Palm Beach on his *Anita Venetian,* he had become—and remained—land-development-minded. While he suffered a depression in the trading markets, he experienced a boom in his bank account from the sale of grapefruit "ranches," orange-grove and winter-home developments. One venture (Mizner Associates), for which he acted as director, sold more than $9,000,000 worth of lots. But when they filed for bankruptcy, two years after formation of the corporation, its assets indicated only $56,000. Where did the money go? Mr. Livermore liked to *live*: so did his promotion-minded friends.

By July, 1927, Jesse Livermore appeared to have faded out of the market; it was as though he had never started down that price-changes road-to-riches, back in 1893. For the moment, at least, he set Cutten aside in his thoughts. Jealousy is the soul's destroyer and while Livermore wasn't actually jealous of Cutten's phenomenal, consistent successes, he did make a mental note to ruin that fellow if the chance ever arose.

Meanwhile, Livermore simply faded out of the news columns. To him, this was a tragedy even more painful than the realization that he wasn't openly connected with Wall Street anymore. But he still owned a seat on the Chicago Board of Trade, he still managed to hang on to *Evermore*—and his ever-loving wife still had the Livermore jewels.

And then, Jesse "wuz robbed."

Chapter 9

"J. L."

At *Evermore,* on a May evening in 1927, the Livermores were entertaining some week-end guests—the
Aronsohns. Harry Aronsohn, an affluent silk-manufac-
turer, was a very special friend to Livermore—a friend,
who could be depended on for help when financial
pressure dictated the need.

After the demi-tasse, the Livermore children, Paul
(age six) and Jesse, Jr. (age nine) went up to bed, while
their parents and guests, in gowns and dinner-jackets,
sipped Benedictines in the drawing room.

Suddenly, the French doors leading to the terrace
burst open, and two well-dressed, masked "dinner rob-
bers" leaped into the room. The Livermores and their
guests were ordered—at gun-point—to freeze. One of
the bandits then softly ordered the women to hand over
their jewelry—and the men their wallets. The other thief
growled an order to Jesse to "open the safe."

"But I can't," the ex-Wall Street king bravely protested. "I can't do it. I haven't my glasses . . ."

What happened then caused Jesse's eyes to widen
with disbelief . . . He had anticipated a few snarls and
blows designed to force him to open the safe; but the
well-prepared robber simply yanked out a hammer and
chisel, proceeded directly to the spot behind a painting
which concealed the wall-safe, and with a few deft
blows—the efficient yegg cracked open the vault. But
all he found inside were some valueless papers. Grit-

ting his teeth, the disappointed burglar leaped upon Livermore, tore off his gold wrist-watch—and his sapphire pinky ring.

At this, Dorothy Livermore cried, "Oh, why do you take his jewelry? I gave them to him for his birthday. Now please give Pops back his ring and watch . . ."

To the amazement of all, Mrs. Livermore's words worked wonders. The thief gallantly handed Livermore back his jewelry. But he did take all the cash (about $200) and other gems from the Livermores and the Aronsohns. Again, Mrs. L—emboldened by her previous success—pleaded with the robbers to return the "baubles" of their guests and to leave them enough for a taxi.

The polite house-breakers, as though hypnotized by Mrs. L., handed the Aronsohns their jewels—and two dollars "for a cab." But the Livermore jewels—including a matched-pearl necklace valued at $60,000—they took with them.

On the following day, Jesse Livermore again made headlines in the *Times.* This time the banner went:

LIVERMORES ROBBED OF $100,000 IN GEMS
AT POINT OF PISTOLS

Of course, this opportunity was just too good for the stock market-minded Livermore to pass up; and so he passed on a few sentiments to an adulating reporter, who wrote accordingly:

> His (Livermore's) operations have about them
> the glamour of youthful daring and adventure
> . . . He traded in everything: Wheat, Cotton,
> Rubber, Industrial stocks and Oils. Sometimes
> he lost heavily, but always escaped . . . much
> of the time in such a way as to startle the
> Street . . .

All that summer and fall, the subsequent chase (by the police, and by Burns Brothers detectives), and the eventual capture and trial of the gem thieves, kept the Livermore name and legend burning bright-as-a-beacon in newspapers all across the land. There was an amusing sidelight to the notorious robbery: one of the crooks admitted having thrown Mrs. Livermore's necklace into the bushes along a stretch of road near Darien, Connecticut . . . Thereupon, the immortal writer of *Topics of the Times* amusingly described activities of the high-class residents of that area, as they eagerly crawled about on hands and knees probing the bushes bordering Boston Post Road for that "necklace in the bush."

It was never found: but the crooks were.

One of them, Arthur Barry, alias Billy Gibson, was sent up for twenty-five years. The other, dashingly nicknamed "Boston Billy," got fifty years at hard labor. And Livermore's trusted chauffeur—Eddie Kane—who had given the thieves "the lay of the land" got off with a lesser sentence.

All the publicity, however, somehow worked wonders on Livermore's cash condition. During the bull market leading to 1929, he managed to profit successfully from partnership accounts. He bought—and, indeed, sailed in a new yacht, the *Atherio II,* costing less, of course, than a million dollars. He even received the nomination on an opposition ticket for Vice-Commodore of the Columbia Yacht Club.

Livermore promptly—and wisely—declined the honor, and the club's regular ticket was elected. The party running on the regular ticket for this post happened to be Livermore's old friend, T. Coleman Du Pont; and Livermore just couldn't run in opposition to such a loyal stalwart.

He was now fifty years old. He was careful in choosing a style of dress to befit his status as a "Wall Street millionaire." A family picture shows him wearing the kind of fedora FDR made famous. Mrs. Livermore, now pressing a plump thirty—and already losing her battle with the bottle—appears in a cloche of the "It Girl" type made famous by Clara Bow. The boys are attired in the customary woolen caps, tweeds and knickers, and long Argyle socks. The Livermores appeared to be a happily domesticated couple, indeed—in spite of the trials of keeping bill-collectors happy—and despite the friction already beginning to develop between Mrs. L. and "J. L." (as everybody, including his family, now addressed the former farmboy). Rumors of reported clandestine romances in hotel rooms while he "was working" caused the friction.

And then "J. L." ran into trouble.

In the spring of 1929, while busily cleaning up in the runaway bull market, Livermore became the target of a number of odious law-suits.

*   *   *   *   *

On April 4th, ninety-three investors—who had suffered through the Boca Raton Crash in 1926—sued Livermore, Du Pont and associates for $1,450,000. Led by the militant son of Henry Morgenthau, former Ambassador to Turkey, the claimants lodged the longest complaint ever filed up to that time, in an abortive effort to recover their losses. Maximilian Morgenthau's complaint ran 870 pages.

Basically, the injured land speculators claimed that the Livermore-led promoters had committed fraud; that they had misrepresented Florida lots; and that they had operated a realty management and sales corporation without any knowledge of the business whatsoever. The plaintiffs went on to say that when the Boca Raton "swindle" had been launched on April 21, 1925, the promoters had appointed as president, Addison Mizner ("an architect without experience in real estate development"). Mizner promptly appointed as secretary of the land company, his brother Wilson (a playwright). Although the suit made a sensational landing in the courts, its later departure (when privately settled) proved quiet and inconspicuous.

*   *   *   *   *

In July of 1929, Livermore became annoyed with a suit lodged against him by the directors and officers of the Carbonite Corporation of America. So incensed was he, that he refused to appear in an examination before trial. But the Court proved to be adamant. The *Times* reported:

> ... Jesse Livermore, former Wall Street speculator, was directed by Supreme Court Justice Walsh to testify before trial against him for $525,000 . . . for alleged breach of an agreement . . .

It was alleged that Livermore had reneged on an agreement to head a group to furnish money to this marginal company by peddling stock to an unsuspecting public.

Again, the suit reached a quiet end after a private settlement was effected—out of court.

*   *   *   *   *

And, of course, there were other annoyances—such as Livermore's having to lose some of his beloved, much-boasted about trappings of wealth. During 1925-1926, he had been forced to sell his town-house on West 76th Street. Now, he lived in an apartment at 817 Fifth Avenue, while his family spent most of their time out at the "estate." His office in the Heckscher Building was but a short walk from the apartment, down the Avenue. The financial community vibrated with rumors that Jesse Livermore had welded together a powerful organization that could move stock prices up and down at will; and like Uncle Dan'l Drew, could make them "wiggle-waggle," too.

Even while Livermore reveled in his power—so reminiscent of old times, those cherished times when the papers had alluded to him as the "Great Bear" . . . when his name had been "feared" in the marketplace —he smelled the oncoming "crash."

*   *   *   *   *

Came October, 1929: Jimmy Walker exerted his winning charm to woo voters away from his rival, Fiorello LaGuardia. Thomas Edison visited his old friend, Henry Ford. And philosopher John Dewey, at seventy, already could see "human motives other than money on the rise . . ."

During the second week of that fateful month, an exceptionally violent decline set in on the Stock Exchange. This sudden set-back, of course, was attributed to the "throwing over of unwieldly speculative holdings by pools and individual adventurers . . ."

Clarence Hudson & Company, then a popular brokerage firm, continued to advertise the alluring slogan, "There is no substitute for safety"—while, at the same time, trying to inveigle more elevator-operators, cabdrivers, and even sweat-shop workers into "putting out a line of long stocks."

On October 21st, in a fervid address before a meeting of the New York Credit Men's Association, Professor Irving Fisher, head of Yale University's Department of Economics, asserted:

". . . Yesterday's break in the market was a

shaking-out of the lunatic fringe that attempts
to speculate on margin . . ."

Professor Fisher further favored the giant trusts (so
soon to go bankrupt) and assured his audience prices
of leading issues were indeed *low.*

In the newspapers, at least, Livermore got his long-
awaited revenge on his bullish rivals—including Cutten.
Referring to Jesse's supposed leadership in driving
stock prices down, the papers said:

. . . Livermore, formerly one of the country's
biggest speculators, is the leader of the bear
clique against Arthur Cutten, leader of the
bulls . . .

For a while, Jesse could get quite a lift from such an
item, and feel as though he were walking on air. Imagine
being publicly heralded as a *victor* over a speculator
like Cutten! And when the newspapers referred to "J.
L." as the "plunging speculator, who—because of the
desperately-driven longs—has run his profits into the
millions," his euphoria couldn't be dispelled. Even the
week-ends at *Evermore*—and the tragic sight of his
blind-drunk wife—failed to depress his high spirits.

The once-beautiful bride of eighteen who had trem-
bled and clung to the arm of her middle-aged bridegroom on that December wedding-evening eleven years
ago, was now an ugly nightmare to him. And Livermore
sought frequent escape from the nightmare—in various
mid-town love-nests, in the arms of well-paid show-girls.

But his love affairs on-the-sly didn't thrill him half as
much as did his love affairs with the press. Nothing was
more exciting to him than reading about himself on
page 1 of *The New York Times.* How he must have
relished this *bon mot,* appearing at the time of the
"great crash":

. . . The ascendancy of Livermore to the position he once held as a leading market operator on the bear-side after years of eclipse is one of the most intriguing developments of the market.

Likened by the imaginative press to a "grand croupier" in a rigged roulette game, the "Great Bear" was alleged to have amassed a multi-million-dollar fortune while people were jumping out of Wall Street windows.

How did the "Great Bull," Arthur Cutten, fare? By mid-November of 1929, he had dropped more than $50,000,000. On the surface, it would seem that Livermore should have been ecstatic with the "revenge" he had wreaked on Cutten. But the facts indicate that his victory was a Pyrrhic one. Even though Livermore had won millions on the short side of the market, he had actually lost about six million in his long position! Incredibly enough, Livermore's losses just about balanced any gains he may have made. The healthy cut he got from the commissions he had generated proved to be a wonderfully reliable sum to fall back on; and besides, he had effectively recouped his lost reputation as a genuine force in the market.

By November 13th, more than thirty billion dollars in the market value of listed securities had washed away. Innumerable banks, trust companies, title-guaranty companies, brokerage houses and thousands upon thousands of misguided, ill-advised people went broke. The debacle proved to be but a prelude, however, to a worsening depression.

Meanwhile, a ray of humor entered Livermore's life when he read about his adversary's wife being "held up" in Chicago . . . Early on a November evening, 1929, Mrs. Cutten and a dear female friend (Mr. Cutten *always* retired at ten) came out of a theatre in the Windy City, and entered the Cutten car—a Pierce Arrow of ancient vintage. (Cutten, of course, wouldn't waste money on Rolls Royces, like Livermore did). Before the chauffeur could turn the ignition-key, a pistol-barrel poked him in the face. Four other well-armed hoods yanked open the car-doors and demanded that Mrs. Cutten hand over "the jewels."

But all the thieves got for their trouble amounted to four dollars from Mrs. Cutten's purse, and about a hundred dollars from the handbag of her less-wealthy companion. The thieves should have known in advance that there would be no jewels, for a man like Arthur Cutten (so unlike his flamboyant and daring counterpart in the City) never squandered money on pearl necklaces or other extravagances.

The counterpart, meanwhile, seemed to be losing much of that "daring" with age. Approaching his fifty-third birthday (as 1929 came to an end, and the 30's quietly came into being), "J. L." took a sad look at his family and at the financial state of his country. Sitting in his favorite speakeasy, an involuntary shudder seized his frame as he reached for another martini, made of the finest bootleg gin. Even though he had failed to make a killing from the crash—as Bernard Baruch did —his thinking was in a similar vein to that of the future adviser of presidents. Indeed, "J. L." also envisioned hard times ahead.

Chapter 10

THE JIGGLERS, THE JUGGLERS

On the heels of the "Great Crash" of 1929, a severe depression gripped America from coast to coast. In the wake of the stock market debacle that had wiped out elevator-operators and boot-blacks—as well as margined millionaires—a great hue and cry for reform of the evils practised in the world of Wall Street pervaded the land.

Leading the dedicated reformers was an ambitious, dynamic politico, who had, in 1929, been soundly drubbed in the mayoralty race in New York City against the popular, but questionably honest, Jimmy Walker. After the crash, Fiorello LaGuardia, the "Little Flower," set out determinedly to win the Mayor's spot and to reform the market in the process. Naturally, another reformer, who was then eyeing the White House, added his condemnation of the privileged position which members of the New York Stock Exchange—who were directors of listed companies, and who also managed the pools in said companies—had over the ordinary investor. But long before Franklin Delano Roosevelt occupied the White House, the machinery to regulate the securities business had been set into motion.

The trigger that exploded the secrecy and skullduggery (legal, of course) on the New York Stock Exchange was an exposé—*The Greatest Era of Crooked Finance*—a book by Watson Washburn and Edmund S. DeLong. These authors decried the frauds floated in the over-the-counter market, where even the "blue sky itself" could be sold to the gullible; and they censured the nefarious practices of the jigglers* and the jugglers* who managed pool operations and other shenanigans on and off the floor of the Exchange.

That spring, a Senate committee held hearings in New York, and subpoenas were issued to the leading jugglers—Percy Rockefeller, Mike Meehan, G. F. Breen, R. F. Hoyt, and a host of others. But of far more interest to the committee, dedicated to finding the reasons the public had been inveigled into the crash, was the testimony of one A. Newton Plummer, a tout-sheet operator.

Fearlessly, Plummer named names and accused the jugglers of buying and selling stocks "to create activity on which they expected to unload their blocks of stock." Helping assiduously in this direction was a host of easily purchasable financial writers for leading newspapers. Of the Wall Street chatterbox who had succeeded Henry Clews, Plummer said, "C. W. Barron possesses a brilliant intellect, an itchy palm, and the worst stock market judgment I ever observed in a big man . . ."

Indeed, the big men of the Street came in for quite a roasting from witnesses hailed before the committee. Samuel Untermyer, declaring that Exchange quotes "control the courts and bank chiefs alike," felt that the government should have regulated the whole industry "from the beginning." Looking back at an Exchange before it cleaned its own house, the reformer reflected, "There was a time . . . when the New York

---

*Jigglers and jugglers were synonymous, except for the degree and scope of their manipulations. Jigglers looked for fast in-and-out moves and quick profits, thus giving the term "jiggle" to any price up-and-down occurring in a period of, say, a week. The jugglers, however, were the price-movers who looked for the long-term and the big-swing. They were the kings of the market at that time.

Stock Exchange was a gambling den and trading on it the worst form of gambling. The bulk of its dealings were not only manipulated but fictitious and a decoy to the public under cover of which the greatest fortunes in the country were accumulated . . ."

Unfortunately for Jesse Livermore, he had never belonged to "the club," and had never been able to accumulate, and hold on to, any great fortune. While the jigglers and the jugglers, the pen-prostitutes and the law-makers were dragged into the harsh light of public scrutiny, it was amazing that Jesse Livermore—now a "skinny trader," a has-been without a large bankroll, who could trade only in 100-share lots—was able to avoid appearing, or giving testimony. What was he doing? According to a latter-day historian,* Livermore was busily operating a string of bucket-shops, even as the law began to lay its heavy hand upon such betting palaces.

Speaking of the market, he said, "Rome wasn't built in a day and no real movement ends in a day or a week . . ." The movement to rid the marketplace of the manipulators took longer than a week, of course; in fact, the movement still continues—and probably will as long as dishonest people infiltrate the market.

But what of the Livermore marriage, a union that was formed with a burning love, and now seemed to be in the process of burning itself out because of the whiskey bottle?

The Livermore marriage had indeed lasted for more than "a day," and its end would take more than "a week." Even though "J. L." himself went on an occasional, and perhaps forgivable, bat (considering his high cost of living and his unending, losing battle to

*Sobel, Dr. Robert, *The Big Board,* Macmillan, 1965.

meet it) he had little patience with—in fact, he just couldn't stand people who hadn't the power to control their habits.

To add to his distress, Mrs. Livermore, in the spring of 1932, became enamored of a prohibition agent named J. Walter Longcope. The first rumblings of a rift in the Livermore marriage appeared in the *Times,* on August 16, 1932:

Mrs. Livermore Hints At Reno Divorce . . .

And a month later, in Reno, Nevada, Mrs. Livermore entered suit against her husband for desertion. The following day, a sympathetic judge handed her her freedom. Five minutes later, she married Longcope—and Jesse was once again a free man. But he wasn't quite free of the bills. He had to pay for the support of his sons, and was even sued for payment of $2,775 by a spurious antiques dealer, who labored under the distressing idea that rich people should pay their bills.

It would seem that Jesse had had enough of marriage after his two ill-fated voyages on the matrimonial seas . . . But on March 28, 1933, the fifty-six-year-old speculator married Harriet Metz Noble, a thirty-eight-year-old widow and an accomplished concert singer. There was no honeymoon. In fact, the bridegroom quickly persuaded his bride to part with more than $136,000 in negotiable securities, which he needed, he said, "for margin." He also had handed his old broker friend, Ben Block, a note in excess of $84,000 to fall due a month after his marriage—and the note had been returned uncollected and protested.

To meet the money demands of his second ex-wife and to try to subsist with his third, Livermore painfully forced himself to give up *Evermore.*

Valued before the auction sale at $1,350,000 (more than $150,000 already had been spent on landscaping alone), this lavishly furnished estate came accoutered with such luxuries as a "$10,000 needlework screen" and a "$22,500 Rolls." When the hammer dropped on the last item of the Livermore estate, the sum that had been realized fell woefully short of his creditors' anticipated proceeds. The house and grounds went for $168,-000; the needlepoint, for $800; and Mrs. W. Guggenheim got a bargain when she plunked down $4,750 for the magnificent Rolls. *In toto,* the auction grossed $225,-100.

Already beset by his dire need for funds (hopes for which had been snuffed out by the disappointing sums raised in the auction—money that had gone to lawyers and to bill-collectors), Livermore was now threatened with something else . . . Some underworld friends of Boston Billy, incensed at the severe sentence he had received, threatened to kidnap Livermore and hold him for ransom. This new fear, he attempted to drown in a whiskey glass (a thin, mist-coated crystal one, always full of icy martinis, very dry—very, very dry).

Livermore now became the target of several annoying law-suits—mostly claims from "gulled brokers." His new marital love-nest, which left a lot to be desired, was severely "shook up" by one suit in particular: from Naida L. Krasnova ("said to be an actress"), who sued him for $250,000 for "breach of promise."

In the ensuing battle with his new wife over this suit, Livermore was so upset that he left the house (an apartment at 1100 Park Avenue, where the newlyweds were now living) and disappeared. Mrs. Livermore No. 3 waited two days for her husband to show up; and then she called the police.

"My husband always calls me every hour on the hour,

when he is away from home," the distracted bride told
the investigating officer, "and I fear something terrible
has happened to him . . ."

The "terrible thing" that happened to him was that—
hemmed in by his clamoring creditors, pestered with
summonses and calls for appearances in law-suit after
law-suit, jeered at in the Street by his peers—Livermore simply cracked up. He hurried off on a Monday
morning to his hide-out in the Hotel Pennsylvania,
where he maintained a room using his old alias "Jesse
Lord." Cloistered and shaking in the darkened room, he
drew a bottle out of his coat and began to drink. The
bender lasted for 26 hours.

Bleary-eyed and ashamed of himself, "J. L." found
he could run, but he just couldn't hide. He drew himself
together with all the nerve he could still summon, and
walked into a police station, boldly blaming his dis-
appearance on "amnesia."

Inebriate, amnesiac, or whatever—Jesse Lauriston
Livermore couldn't quite drink away the changes already taking place in the markets.

"Caveat Emptor wasn't only for Romans," was his
eternal credo from the time he first came to Wall Street,
shortly after the turn of the century. And it was in this
spirit of letting the buyer beware that Livermore had
cut his first million from the drop in Anaconda. But on
May 30, 1933, the new Securities Bill became effective
on all new issues; and the psychology of the Street
was changed to "let the seller beware."

Regulation of trading on the exchanges swiftly followed; and Jesse had little hope of making a comeback
based upon his previous practices. Pool operations became outlawed, and even trading on the commodities
exchanges became restricted when the Secretary of
Agriculture, Henry Wallace, invoked provisions of the

1920 futures trading act to hamstring Grain speculators.

Even the master spirit, Arthur Cutten (described by Secretary Wallace as "one of our greatest supporters of the law of supply and demand and *laissez faire*") found it almost impossible to make a few honest dollars through "fictitious and dummy accounts and false reports." "Imagine!" snorted Cutten, "They want me to report all positions over 500,000 bushels! Why, they might as well tell me how much I can sell my horse for. 50,000,000 bushels of Wheat a year is but a beginning with the kind of trading I do . . ."

But Cutten's outbursts against the new bureaucracy didn't move Secretary Wallace one whit. In the spring of 1934, he moved to suspend trading privileges for Cutten on all Grain exchanges in the country.

Meanwhile, Livermore—ex-juggler reduced to the insignificant status of jiggler—couldn't wish away the law-suits besieging him on all sides.

On January 9, 1934, J. J. Tierney won judgment on a $10,000 note held by J. R. Williston (now deceased). The interest costs ran it up to $13,130. Less than a month later, Ben Block won $90,840 judgment against his old friend in connection with the $84,284 "loan" made to Livermore back in 1932.

And so it went. One after another, shafts of misfortune struck and quivered in his flaccid body until there remained only two outs: bankruptcy or suicide.

Livermore still had a lot of "life" in him, so suicide was out . . . "I never quit," he bragged; "I'll make my come-back." And so he chose the bankruptcy route filing his formal petition on March 4, 1934. His sorry condition was reflected in $2,259,212 worth of debts, with an offset of $184,000 in questionable assets.

A few days after his petition broke into print, Jesse received official notice of his suspension as a member of the Chicago Board of Trade. It now became apparent that Livermore's defeat in the markets had been thorough—and complete. In Wall Street—and in LaSalle Street (Chicago)—it appeared that Jesse Livermore was finished. And it would seem that for the rest of his life, he would remain a burnt-out Wall Street memory.

Upon investigating the ex-speculator's assets, the referee found that Livermore's portfolio was made up of a few "cats and dogs," that he had shifted his remaining annuity ($100,000) to his current wife; and that according to his secretary, N. C. Finninger, Mr. Livermore had nothing—not a single red cent. Evidently, however, he still had some anonymous friends, some unshakeable believers in the Livermore ability to make a come-back.

And so it wasn't too surprising when the "penniless" promoter handed a press release to the *Times* saying that he was taking his wife abroad for a "belated wedding trip"—in order to study the European commodity markets. "I've made come-backs before," he confidently assured the reporters, "and I'll do it again . . ." Brave words . . . words that might have come true, if the times had been different.

In the wake of the 1929 panic, the economic condition of the country sank to the nadir of the depression. FDR's bank holiday and the efflorescence of Federal agencies such as the NRA, the WPA, and even the CCC, were desperately foisted upon the citizenry in an attempt to shake our country out of its abortive economic morass. As the Roosevelt administration brought America back to its economic "feet," how did Livermore—a single human being, who also needed financial resuscitation—fare?

In one of his many "reforms," Mr. Roosevelt had seen

to it that his old friend, Joseph P. Kennedy, headed up the first SEC. Manipulative devices, such as wash sales and illegal crosses, were outlawed. In a word, the regulatory door had just about slammed shut in the faces of the market manipulators. The Exchange cleaned house. And even the curb market went off the Street into a sumptuous building, later the home of the American Stock Exchange. Quite apparently, Livermore would never again be able to make a killing from trading in the market (stock prices moved far too slowly during the depression), or by running a specific issue (now an outlawed practice). By 1935, the war on the bucket-shops had flamed to great intensity in New York City; and Jesse didn't exactly relish the thought of being nabbed in a raid on one of the places he allegedly managed—and sent to Sing-Sing.

But he had to make a living somehow . . . So he began to cast about for a clientele whose money he could manage, and thus, hopefully, manage to stay alive himself. There would be his fees for handling these discretionary accounts—and, of course, the under-the-table split-commissions of the old (and wearing) days before his big market plays.

In order to succeed as an investment-account manager, Jesse needed *winners.* To the uninitiated, this might not seem so difficult for a man who had spent a lifetime trying to perfect a stock market system. On the surface it might appear that a man who knew *everything* about the market—from the philosophy of the suckers to the devious techniques of the "boys on the floor" —should have had a better-than-ordinary chance to make money consistently. For a while, Jesse did.

His success hinged on a *unique* system. Basically, his forecasting prowess depended upon a black cat. . . . At that time, Bernie Chipman, manager of the Washington, D. C., office of Laidlaw & Company, owned a black cat which he had picked up and adopted when it was a starving kitten. It was during the depression, Chipman recalled, and "I was broke and three weeks behind in the rent. The brokerage business was so poor, I owed everybody. I was eating fish when the black kitty arrived at my back door. I took her in after wincing from those piercing 'meows.' And right after that I made $1,400 in Westinghouse."

On one of Livermore's occasional visits to the Chipman diggings, he was told what good luck the cat had brought to the impoverished manager; so he began to use the animal as a "signal."

Chipman explained, "The cat, an animal of easy friendship, was forever having kittens. Every time she had a litter, I wired Mr. Livermore in New York and he reversed himself. The first time this happened, he was short. When he got my wire, he covered—and made a cool million. Had he waited, he would have been slaughtered by the bulls."

"Invariably," continued Chipman, "he made money every time I wired him that the cat had kittens. And when I one day wired him that the cat was dead—he fainted!"*

*   *   *   *

Often, when a man is harassed by the worrisome problems of making a living, all his mundane trials can be superseded suddenly by one tragic tribulation that strikes at the heart itself. . . . In the midst of his heroic efforts to keep his body, his Rolls, his yacht and his third marriage together, Jesse Livermore suddenly learned his favorite son had been shot.

---

*A Talisman Cat, Wall Street Journal, November 30, 1940.

Oddly enough, the boy—then sixteen—almost died from a bullet fired at close range into his body by his own *mother!*

This near-tragedy occurred in the living-room of the Santa Barbara (Montecito) home that Dorothy Fox Wendt Livermore Longcope occupied with her two sons after she had shed herself of the ex-prohibition agent. To ensure that her younger, thirteen-year-old son, Paul Alexander, would receive proper schooling, the mother (who had been Mrs. Livermore No. 2) had hired a personable tutor named D. B. Neville, who stayed on at the house as her fiancé.

On Thanksgiving Eve, 1935, drunken Dorothy and her current lover were living it up, taking fast turns at the cocktail-shaker, when Jesse Junior suddenly shouted, "I'm going to get sodden drunk so Mother will know how it looks and will stop her drinking . . ." Upon which, young Livermore snatched up a quart of Golden Wedding and began pouring the fiery stuff down his gullet.

"I'd rather see you dead than drinking!" screamed his half-stoned mother. Without a word, Jesse Jr. dropped the bottle and rushed out of the room. A few moments later he returned, brandishing a shot-gun. "Go ahead," he ranted, holding out the gun to his mother, "go ahead and shoot me. You don't have the nerve . . ."

Neville jumped up from the couch and wrested the gun from the hand of the half-hysterical young man. Junior then whirled about, ran back into the gun-room and quickly returned, waving a loaded .22-rifle. Nimbly dodging the clawing hands of his mother's lover, young Jesse shoved the weapon into her hands—and she pulled the trigger!

"Oh, my God!" Dorothy screamed as her son slumped bloodily to the floor, "I've shot my son . . . He dared me . . ."

The boy was rushed to the hospital; and with the bullet dangerously lodged in his right lung, he hovered between life and death.

"J. L.," meanwhile, was in Saint Louis, trying heroically to make a few honest, SEC-supervised, dollars in some quickie trades. His distress at the news of the shooting soon gave way to fury. . . . "If my son dies," he gritted ominously to newsmen, "I'll spend every cent to see that she (his mother) gets what's coming to her . . ."

Fortunately for all concerned, the young man did not die. For months and months, he suffered a series of critical operations until the bullet was finally removed. (Today, he dreams of writing his own version of his father's life, and plans to include the more titillating escapades with Jesse's ever-available females).

Having sweated out his son's brush with death, Jesse was now beset from a different direction. Uncle Sam suddenly demanded his due—that is, monies due the Revenue cash-register. Livermore had some slight satisfaction in seeing his arch-enemy, Cutten, also harassed by an inexorable Administration. Cutten, who had beaten Secretary Wallace in the courts, now beat the Revenue Bureau. But the effort wore him plumb out; the hard pine-knot from the Canadian woods died in 1936.

Livermore, however, lost his money-fight with the Administration, to the tune of an $800,000 assessment. What methods he found to pay off this staggering sum lie confidentially in the files of the Revenue Bureau. But with Cutten dead, Livermore again came to life in the commodity markets.

By the summer of 1937, he had gleaned enough from Grain-trading to charter a yacht, the *Rogist.* His new burgee, a pure white pennant with the red script *"Nina"* (his pet name for his present wife) fluttered in the breeze, as Jesse took the *Rogist's* wheel into his expert hands and sailed out past Coney Island, for Montauk, Long Island—and some long-neglected deep-sea fishing.

Chapter 11

TWILIGHT BATTLE

July 4, 1937, had to be the happiest day of Jesse Livermore's life. On that beautiful day there shimmered in the sun more than seventy yachts, at anchorage in the sheltered cove off the Montauk Yacht Club. With the aplomb of a French monarch, "Lord Livermore" had chartered Captain John Sweeting's fishing-boat, the *Ranger*—to treat his guests to the thrills of deep-sea fishing.

At about 2:00 in the afternoon, while trolling between Block Island and the Montauk Light, the keen-eyed captain spotted the fin of a giant broadbill. Livermore, aglow with excitement, had himself strapped into the fishing-chair. He wrapped his lithe, eager fingers firmly around the baseball-bat-thick haft of a huge rod bearing a Pfleuger 10/0 reel, housing hundreds of yards of 36-pound test cuttyhunk. Carefully, expertly, the captain skittered the tantalizing bait near the monster's nose. Suddenly, the swordfish struck! And the fight was on. . .

That fight lasted over an hour—but Jesse won. The exhausted, but exhilarated conqueror stared with boyish awe at the giant broadbill being hoisted aboard by block-and-tackle. "J. L.'s" catch, weighing 486 pounds, remains the second-largest ever caught off Montauk on rod-and-reel. Heady with success, the speculator-sportsman basked in the warm praise of his guests; and one sycophant went so far as to say, "J. L., since you're such a fine fisherman, why don't you write a book about it? I'll bet it would be a smash!"

It was a simple suggestion—but it stunned Livermore. Could it be that, quite by accident, he had just been handed the key to a possible new fortune? With this challenging thought racing through his mind, he smiled kindly at his well-wisher and countered, "Why should I write a book about deep-sea fishing? How many people really can afford the sport? But someday, I may write a book on a subject many people ought to know about— a book on how to make a success out of speculation. After all, I did sort of develop a system for my half-century battle with the bulls. . . ."

So began Jesse Lauriston Livermore's last battle, his twilight battle, to recoup riches and stock market renown. It didn't take too much convincing to obtain a contract from a reputable publisher. Livermore's problem was, what kind of a system could he concoct that would be both convincing and confusing at the same time? He, more than anyone else in stock market history, knew well the bitter meaning of the maxim, "If there is any easy money lying around Wall Street, no one is going to put it into your pocket."

But he felt he also knew something about people: that they are, by instinct, suckers; that they dream of, and are willing to pay for a magic method of forecasting stock prices. And so he formulated the "Livermore Key."

Patterned after the Dow Theory (then, as now, followed by thousands of forecast-minded devotees of the tape), the Livermore Key depended upon signals from two stocks in each of four representative groups. The Dow followers, of course, use Rails to check the action of Industrials. Livermore decided to use the price action of the leaders to check each other.

Naturally, Jesse Livermore never did anything halfway. He took a luxurious suite in the Squibb Building, at 745 Fifth Avenue, where (according to Gerald Loeb) he had a room with boards lining the walls. And he had several boys there to mark-up the boards with colored chalk, thus giving visitors the impression important calculations were occurring.

And while waging his endless fight to make expensive ends meet, Livermore began to work out his key system. Patiently, and doggedly, he prepared his "secrets" of stock market success. He was encouraged, of course, by the hope that when his book burst upon the investing scene, those who still revered his name would gobble up the work in great numbers—so great that he would promptly regain his lost millions, or at least, be able to pay some of his debts, which were mounting by the minute.

By March, 1940, Livermore's literary labor-pains were over, and his brain-child was finally delivered. Ever public relations-minded, "J. L." threw a buffet dinner to launch his opus, making certain to invite the leading financial writers and book reviewers. He was to learn— soon and bitterly—that adulation from literary people comes hard; and that usually, a book's success in the stores depends more on what lies between its covers than on the slant of its promotion.

At publication time, the book was mentioned in *The New York Times,* which grudgingly acknowledged the ex-Cotton King's effort in a few words:

> . . . Jesse Livermore, of 745 Fifth Avenue, a fre-
> quently spectacular operator . . . has written a
> book entitled: "How to Trade in Stocks" . . .

On Sunday, March 10th, however, Livermore had the pleasure of reading a story occupying the first column on page 1 of the Financial Section of the *Times.* The column was written by the late and immortal Burton Crane, who, in discussing Livermore's book, observed in a tongue-in-cheek manner that the book attempted to put over "a new trading plan." To be sure, Livermore couldn't convince or prove to Mr. Crane that the *Key* was indeed workable.

Workable or not, the Livermore book couldn't have appeared at a more inopportune time. The United States had just about roused itself from the morass of a long depression; and the citizenry had just about become acclimated to a renewal of its faith in banks. But the brokerage business still had a long, long way to go before it could lure the public into "investing in a share of American business." In brief, Livermore's glittering hope for financial succor through book-royalties died a sudden death with his first royalty statement. Like the Wall Street of 1929, his literary effort "laid an egg."

On the afternoon preceding Thanksgiving Eve of 1940, "J. L." sat quietly on a stool at the men's bar in the Sherry-Netherland Hotel. His ever-moving fingers aimlessly twirled the stem of his glass (his second martini in ten minutes); and, as if in a hypnotic trance, he stared fixedly at the rotating glass. He reviewed, over and over in his mind, the money-merry-go-round of his life. Oh, yes . . . The money was always there in Wall Street. He just hadn't held on to it when he had it.

As he sat there rolling the half-empty glass back and forth, his coups and his failures passed before him in fleeting review. He felt as though he were watching a bad movie. . .

Now the memory of the previous evening loomed startlingly before him. He and Nina (who called him "Laurie") had been happily sipping cocktails at the Stork. As they waited for the maitre d' to approach with the dinner menu, Don Arden, the Stork Club photographer, came over and politely asked permission to take a picture. "Go right ahead," Jesse said graciously.

"Take my picture for the last time. Tomorrow I am going away. . ."

Nina looked at her husband with alarm; but he patted her hand reassuringly and told her he was only kidding. But was he?

He asked himself this question now, as he sat on the bar stool at the Sherry-Netherland; and suddenly, he reached an irrevocable decision. Livermore dug into his vest-pocket and fished out the ever-present gold pencil. From his coat-pocket, he produced a notebook, plopped it on the polished bar-top, and began to write.

First, he totaled up his debts—all $365,000 of them. Shuddering inwardly, he wondered how in the world he would ever be able to amass such a staggering sum—especially with all those damn new SEC rules and regulations hamstringing market manipulation.

"Another one, Mr. Livermore?" asked the solicitous bartender. But "J. L." ignored the white-coated figure as though it didn't exist.

Then he began to write a long, long note to his wife. It began, "Dear Nina . . ."—and rambled on for eight pages. All through the note was the recurrent theme: MY LIFE HAS BEEN A FAILURE . . . MY LIFE HAS BEEN A FAILURE . . . MY LIFE . . .

His life had always been lived in style—with flair, with élan that made him a talked-about figure in homes all over the nation—and, indeed, around the world.

Oh, yes. Jesse Livermore—almost all his life—had been news. He could hardly envision a commonplace death for himself—a quiet natural demise, meriting a one-paragraph item on the obituary page. Nearing the end of his long note, he wrote, "My life has been a failure . . ." But he had no intention of ending it that way.

Wall Street history reveals that the great men of the

Street, when tired of fighting, simply blew their brains out. Perhaps Jessie Livermore now wanted to show the world that he was as much a man as Charles Barney (former president of the defunct Knickerbocker Trust), who bravely shot himself to death, rather than face the public outcry when Hettie Green caused his bank to go under, in the financial deluge of 1907.

On the afternoon of November 28, 1940, as the sun dipped below the Palisades looming over the Hudson, Jesse Livermore ended his last note—and signed it: "Laurie." As always, he was impeccably attired—in a grey flannel suit, fairly new shoes, a light blue tab-collar shirt and navy foulard tied into the newest dimple-knot. Carefully, he slipped off his spectacles and set them into their leather case; then he placed the case into the inside pocket of his jacket. Dabbing the slight sweat from his forehead, Jesse slowly straightened up from his stool and, with a measured walk, headed toward the Sherry-Netherland men's room.

For several years, rumor-mongers had linked him romantically with the gorgeous red-head who checked hats at this famous hostelry. It was also bruited about Broadway that Jesse intended to make that comely lass Mrs. Livermore No. 4 sometime soon (as soon as he could conveniently rid himself of Mrs. L. No. 3).

"Success," he had said, and said again, "rides on the hour of decision." His hour was now at hand. . . .

But his decision to use the men's room underwent a sudden change. Abruptly—and unnoticed—the tired speculator ducked into the hat-check girl's domain, and dropped like a sack into a handy chair there at the rear. Uncontrollably, his heart hammered and his hand shook as though he had palsy. After a few moments, the tremors subsided and his heart slowed—just enough. Then in one swift motion, he drew a pistol, held it to his temple and pulled the trigger.

At 5:30 P.M., Jesse Livermore, Jr. stood stoically over his father's crumpled corpse and calmly made the identification. With all the drama of a stage tragedy, the Livermore life had reached a climactic end. Nothing now remained but a legend—and a legacy.

Livermore's end—like Balzac's—was pathetic and touching. He, too, died "burnt out by his desires, drained dry . . . the victim of his own works." He had wanted everything—fame and fortune—and he had won them all. He left behind an undying legend of stock market sagacity which time (and the truth) can never erase. Most people, after all, believe in the Pirandello aphorism: "If you believe it is so—it's so."

So much for the legend of Jesse L. Livermore. And now to his legacy: "The Livermore Key."

PART III

THE LIVERMORE LEGACY

"You can win a horse race;
but you can't beat the races . . ."
. . . . Anonymous.

Chapter 12

THE LIVERMORE KEY

Long before he blew out his brains, Jesse Livermore unwittingly followed Pope's immortal advice:

> Get place and wealth, if possible
>> with grace;
> If not, by any means, get wealth
>> and place . . .

And the "means" he chose (hopefully, the key to *his* wealth and place) was his book, *How to Trade in Stocks,* which offered to a gullible public the famous (but fantasy) Livermore Key to stock market success.

In the years following the arrival of the SEC, Livermore's manipulative strategies ended. His lack of capital and the loss of his reputation on the Street had relegated him to the "has-been" class, in the opinion of the knowing ones on Manhattan's "toe." Livermore hoped his "literary" effort would rectify all this; that through it, he would not only recapture his wealth, but his reputation—*and* his following.

At the time Livermore concocted his "Key," the suckers who speculated were enamored with two plans, in particular, for trading success: the Buchalter Plan and the Burlinghame Plan.

Basically, the Buchalter concept confined itself to commodities, a field that—with the CEA controls on futures—could hardly attract a broad clientele.

The Burlinghame Plan, however, fascinated Jesse.

In essence, this Plan represented a sophisticated, professionally-managed opportunity for investors who were too busy or too lazy to manage their own accounts. The Burlinghame people were shrewd enough, of course, not to divulge their system's secrets to the general investing public. Instead, the suckers were invited to open accounts of a discretionary nature with certain Exchange firms. The customer's men handling these accounts were provided with limited powers of attorney (they could make trading decisions, but couldn't withdraw securities or money from the accounts). Then, the customer's men executed orders received directly from the Plan's main office in Boston.

(How successful—or unsuccessful—the Burlinghame Plan eventually turned out to be might make an interesting thesis for a master's degree candidate).

But Livermore, who had left school at fourteen, cared little for theories or educational exercises. It was the *bottom line* that counted with him. And he clearly envisioned how wonderful it would be for him—even *with* the SEC—to sit at the center of a huge fan-of-clients spread out over the country, which could create *distribution* (taking stock out of the market and selling it into the hands of shareholders, who would then transfer the shares to their own names and lock them away in safe-deposit boxes for their heirs). So Livermore conceived his book (designed to take the speculating out of speculation), in the hope that enough well-heeled investors would buy it, become confused by its "simple system," and so turn to him to handle their money.

Ever the strategist, Livermore persuaded his publisher to print two editions simultaneously. The deluxe edition (limited)—a handsome, leather-bound affair that sold for $5—was the one Livermore was interested in; its purchasers, obviously, would be the relatively scarce number of rich people still interested in the stock market. The regular "anyman's" edition sold for half the price, $2.50. With this bit of background material concerning Livermore's true motives in becoming an author, here is the essence of his "Key" . . .

Knowing that the most popular forecasting theory employed in Wall Street at the time was the Dow Theory, Livermore cleverly patterned his Key to embody similar features. As most informed readers of latter-day financial pages already know, the Dow method uses the Rail Index to check the action of the Industrials. Thus, if the Industrials rise, and the Rails rise, the theorist has had a "confirming signal." If the Industrials sag and the Rails rise, the theorist waits.

In a shrewd attempt to combine the elements of time and price into a logical, simple-sounding system, Livermore used two leading stocks from each of the four main industries then being traded on the New York Stock Exchange.

In the Steels, he selected "Bessie" (Bethlehem Steel) and "Big Steel" (United States Steel); in the Aircraft section of the list, Douglas and United Aircraft; in Mail Order, Sears and "Monkey" (Montgomery Ward); and in Motors, General Motors and Chrysler.

In brief, Livermore selected an arbitrary number of points indicating a move from what he called his "pivotal price." Suppose this "Key price" was $49 for "Big Steel," and $90 for "Bessie" . . . Now, say, both stocks moved up six points each, or a total of twelve points (Livermore didn't strictly adhere to both stocks moving precisely six points each; one could have moved five, and the other seven, to make his twelve-point step). Livermore would then ink the resultant prices on specially prepared columnar-ruled paper. He used blue ink

On June 20th, the price of U. S. Steel was recorded in the Secondary Rally column. Refer to Explanatory Rule 6-G.

On June 24th, prices of U. S. Steel and Bethlehem Steel were recorded in black ink in the Upward Trend column. Refer to Explanatory Rule 5-A.

On July 11th, prices of U. S. Steel and Bethlehem Steel were recorded in the Natural Reaction column. Refer to Explanatory Rules 6-A and 4-A.

On July 19th, prices of U. S. Steel and Bethlehem Steel were recorded in the Upward Trend column in black ink because those prices were higher than the last prices that were recorded in those columns. Refer to Explanatory Rule 4-B.

CHART THREE

	SECONDARY RALLY	NATURAL RALLY	UPWARD TREND	DOWNWARD TREND	NATURAL REACTION	SECONDARY REACTION	SECONDARY RALLY	NATURAL RALLY	UPWARD TREND	DOWNWARD TREND	NATURAL REACTION	SECONDARY REACTION	SECONDARY RALLY	NATURAL RALLY	UPWARD TREND	DOWNWARD TREND	NATURAL REACTION	SECONDARY REACTION
				38						40						78		
		49						52						101				
					39 1/4					39 3/4							79	
1938							46 1/2											
DATE			U. S. STEEL						BETHLEHEM STEEL						KEY PRICE			
JUNE 17																		
SAT. 18																		
20	45 3/8						48 1/4						93 5/8					
21	46 1/2						49 7/8						96 3/8					
22	48 1/2						50 7/8						99 3/8					
23		51 1/4						53 1/4						104 1/2				
24			53 3/4						55 1/8						108 7/8			
SAT. 25			54 7/8						58 1/8						113			
27																		
28																		
29			56 7/8						60 1/8						117			
30			58 3/8						61 5/8						120			
JULY 1			59												120 5/8			
SAT. 2			60 7/8						62 1/2						123 3/8			
5																		
6																		
7			61 3/4												124 1/4			
8																		
SAT. 9																		
11					55 5/8						56 3/4						112 3/8	
12					55 1/2												112 1/4	
13																		
14																		
15																		
SAT. 16																		
18																		
19			62 3/8						63 1/8						125 1/2			
20																		
21																		
22																		
SAT. 23																		
25			63 1/4												126 3/8			
26																		
27																		
28																		
29																		

for the upward movements, and red ink for the downward.

A brief glance at a sample record-sheet taken from Livermore's book (with the kind permission of Duell, Sloan and Pearce and Investor's Press) indicates clearly how Livermore kept his records.

As to what significance this method could have in today's market, no one can factually say. Livermore himself said, "All my life I've been a 60-40 player, content to clear my 20%." But who can believe even this? So lest any reader acquire the wrong impression—that this discussion of the Livermore system is in any way an endorsement—please remember what Arthur Cutten (a very sharp—and highly successful speculator, who retired from the Wall Street wars with many millions) observed: "Anybody who really made money in the market wouldn't go around telling anybody else how he did it."

Jesse Livermore did make millions. But he lost them all—and then some. In his half-hearted attempt to tell people how to trade in the stock market, he used fancy-sounding ploys like "Natural Reactions," "Natural Rallies," "Pivotal Points" and more.

But obviously, his system's strict dependency upon price movements precludes the fundamental factors often causing price changes—factors which even today's technicians are beginning to look into seriously: level of earnings, security of the dividend, merger possibilities, and much, much more. Oh, yes. On the floor of the New York Stock Exchange, on the floor of the American Stock Exchange, and on the floor of the country's fourteen Regional Stock Exchanges, charts do not make the prices, systems do not make the prices: people do.

So long as people rush headlong into speculative attempts to profit from price changes, just so long will

Jesse Livermore's wistful comment remains true: "Wall Street is always the same: only the pockets change."*

*(also attributed to Gertrude Stein.)

THE FOUR FACES
OF JESSE LIVERMORE

"J. L." Master Market Manipulator.

He bulled up Seneca Copper, Koster Radio, Mexican Pete, and Piggly-Wiggly. Envied, hated, feared, he was respectfully referred to as "J. L."

JESSE LIVERMORE: Millionaire

Pictured just after he had made his third multi-million market comeback, Jesse Livermore had become a legend on the Street. He was a member of the New York Curb and The Chicago Board of Trade. But he could never realize a life-long ambition to become a member of the New York Stock Exchange.

JESSE LIVERMORE: Investment Advisor

The toll and strain of fighting the tape for almost a half-century clearly shows on the third face of Jesse Livermore. Ruined in the market by Arthur Cutten, Livermore attempted to make a comeback by becoming an investment advisor and authoring a book: How To Trade In Stocks; The Livermore Key, *Investor's Press Reprint, 1966.*

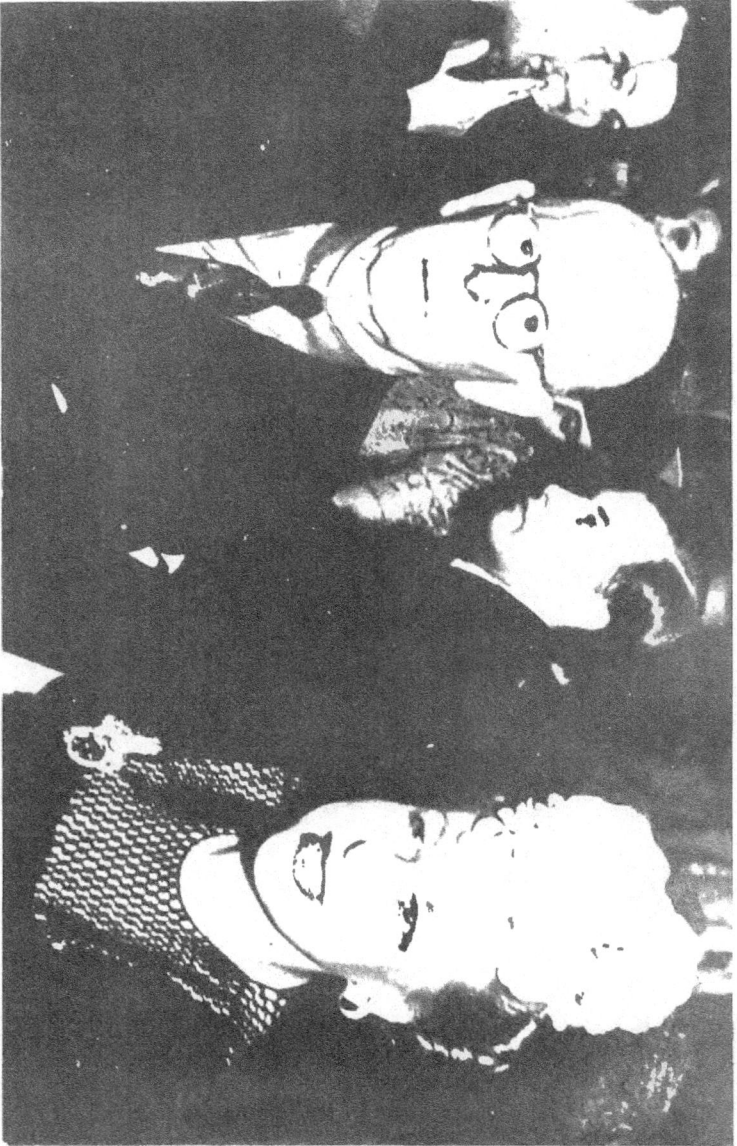

GOOD NIGHT Speculator-King:

Sitting next to his third wife, the Speculator-King permits Stork Club photographer to take one last picture. The following afternoon, in true movie tradition, he committed suicide—and once again made front page headlines.

BIBLIOGRAPHY

BOOKS:

Barron, C., *They Told It To Barron,* New York, 1921
_____, *More They Told It To Barron,* New York, 1924
Livermore, Jesse Lauriston & Le-Fevre, Edwin, *Reminiscences of a Stock Market Operator,* Doran & Co., 1923; *reprint:* Traders Press, Inc., Greenville, S.C. 1985
Livermore, Jesse Lauriston, *How To Trade In Stocks,* Duell, Sloan and Pearce, New York, 1940; *reprint:* Investors Press, Inc., Palisades Park, New Jersey, 1966

ARTICLES:

American Magazine, June, 1920
American Mercury, November, 1928
Business Week, March 12, 1930
Harper's Weekly, December 20, 1913
Literary Digest, April 22, 1922
_____, June 23, 1923
_____, March 30, 1925
_____, October 25, 1930
_____, June 25, 1931
_____, January 2, 1932
Nation, The, September 30, 1909
_____, March 15, 1919
_____, November 13, 1929
_____, March 9, 1932
The New Yorker, "Annals of Finance," John Brooks, June 6, 1959

New Republic, October 22, 1930
Newsweek, December 9, 1940
North American Magazine, January, 1929
_____, March, 1930
Review of Reviews, January, 1926
Saturday Evening Post, January 4, 1930
_____, January 11, 1930
Time Magazine, December 9, 1935
_____, December 9, 1940

NEWSPAPERS:

Commercial & Financial Chronicle
The New York Times:
   1922/23/24/25
   1926/27/28/29
   1932/33/34/37/40
   Reprinted by Permission
The New York World
The Wall Street Journal
Police Gazette

INTERVIEWS:

Gerald Loeb
Henry Peers
Julie Brasz
Al Hartig
C. Halliwell Duell (Telephone)
Court Gerstman
Anonymous Wall Streeters—
   Seven

Acknowledgments

No biographer can really call the book he writes his own. In this case, I have been helped by many friends in my efforts to learn enough about Jesse Lauriston Livermore to bring back his life and career as they were. In this connection I wish to thank Gerald Loeb, of E. F. Hutton; Court Gerstman of Laird, Bissell & Meeds; Henry Peers, of Goodbody & Company; Al Hartig, of Gruntal; Julie Brasz, a Put & Call broker, who came down to the Street in 1906 and remembers Livermore vividly. I also wish to thank those kindly, and ever-young, customer's men and partners who provided me with information, but wish to remain anonymous.

I would be remiss indeed if I didn't thank Lillian Fauci of *The New York Times* Microfilm Department, and the staff at the Hofstra University Library, for their patience and help. I also thank Mrs. Oscar Jurrist, of the Oceanside (New York) Free Library for her help, and Anthony Grech, Reference Librarian of the Association of the Bar of the City of New York for his aid and cogent suggestions.

Finally, I wish to beg forgiveness from my wife and three sons for bringing Jesse Lauriston Livermore into our house to "live" for the past year.

> Paul Sarnoff,
> Oceanside, New York
> Spring, 1967

INDEX

A

American Stock Exchange, 101
Anaconda Copper stock, 40
Anita Venetian, Livermore's yacht,
42, 47, 81
Arden, Don, photographer, 110
Aronsohn, Mr. & Mrs. Harry,
Livermore's friends, 83, 84
Atherio II, Livermore's yacht, 85
Atlantic, George Gould's yacht, 42

B

Baldwin Locomotive stock, 79
Balzac, Honore, author, 113
Barlow, Magistrate Peter B., 60
Barney, Charles, banker, 112
Barron, C. W., market mouthpiece,
94
Barry, Arthur, thief, 85
Baruch, Bernard, trader, 53, 56,
59, 91
Belmont, Perry, trader, 3
Bird Dogs, 53
Black Cat System, 101-102
Blind Pools, 63
Block, Benjamin, stockbroker, 48,
54, 96
Block, Maloney & Company,
stockbrokers, 54
Book of Revelations, 73
Boston Billy, thief, 85
"Boy Plunger," Livermore
sobriquet, 20, 46
Brady, James, bon vivant, 43
Breen, G. F., trader, 94
Bretton Hall Hotel, 48
Buchalter Plan, 117

Bucket Shops, 20-24, 101;
explained, 4
Bull Pool, 81
Burlinghame Plan, 117
Burns Brothers, detectives, 85

C

Carbonite Corporation, 87
Chicago Board of Trade, 76, 82,
100
Chipman, Bernie, manager, 102
Clews, Henry, broker, 94
Columbia Yacht Club, 42, 85
Commodity speculation, 44-45
Connolly, F. A. & Company,
stockbrokers, 56
Corners, 67 (Piggly-Wiggly), 77
(wheat)
Corsair, J. P. Morgan's yacht, 42
Cotton, 46, 49, 81
"Cotton King," Livermore's
sobriquet, 46, 49, 81
Crane, Burton, financial writer,
109, 110
Cutten, Arthur, "The Great Bull,"
74-80, 82, 89, 90, 99, 104;
cited, 76, 79
Cutten, Mrs. Arthur, 90

D

DeForest Radio, Livermore vehicle,
72
DeLong, Edmund S., author, 93
Doheny, E. L., oil operator, 71
Dow Theory, 108, 119
Drew, Daniel, manipulator, 88;
cited, 38

Duell, Sloan and Pearce,
    publishers, 122
DuPont, T. Coleman, realty
    operator, 54, 85

E

Edison, Thomas A., inventor, 88
Evermore, Livermore's estate, 65,
    80, 82, 89, 96

F

Fall, Hon. Albert, Secretary of the
    Interior, 69, 71
Finlay Barrel & Company,
    stockbrokers, 55
Finninger, N. C., Livermore's
    secretary, 100
Fisher, Professor Irving,
    economist, 88; cited, 88-89
Fisk, James, Jr., manipulator, 63
Ford, Henry, industrialist, 88
"Four Horsemen," stock market
    sobriquet, 55
Franklin, Benjamin, printer, 75
Freeport Texas stock, 81

G

Gadfly, Livermore's yacht, 72, 80
Gates, John, gambler, 54
Give-ups, explained, 54
Gould, George J., capitalist, 42
Gould, Jay, manipulator, 79
Great Northern Railway stock, 39
Green, Mrs. Hetty, miser, 112
Guggenheim, Mrs. W., housewife,
    97

H

Harding Memorial Fund, 70
Heckscher Building, 87
How To Trade In Stocks, Livermore
    book available from Investors
    Press, 117

Hoyt, R. F., trader, 94
Hudson, Clarence & Company,
    stockbrokers, 88
Hutton, E. F., stockbroker, 43, 53
Hutton, E. F. & Company,
    stockbrokers, 54, 56

I

Internal Revenue Service, 104

J

Jerome, W. Travers, attorney-
    at-law, 58
Jigglers, explained, 94n
Jordan, Nettie, Mrs. Livermore #1,
    24, 58
Jugglers, explained, 94n

K

Kane, Edward, Livermore's
    chauffeur, 85
Keene, James R., manipulator, 39
Kennedy, President John F., 41
Kennedy, Joseph P., SEC
    Commissioner, 101
Knickerbocker Trust Company,
    112
Krasnova, Naida L., plaintiff, 97

L

La Guardia, Mayor Fiorello, 88, 93
Laidlaw & Company, stockbrokers,
    102
Lawson, Thomas W., manipulator,
    29, 31, 32, 33, 36, 55, 56
Lewisohn Brothers, investment
    bankers, 54, 65, 66
Lewisohn, Walter, investment
    banker, 65
Le Fevre, E., author, 22, 23
Livermore, Hiram E., Jesse
    Livermore's father, 13
Livermore, Jesse Lauriston; cited,
    8, 9, 10, 11, 24, 27, 34, 66, 69, 71,
    78, 88, 95, 104; birth, 13; young
    years, 14-15; at thirty, 36-37; at

fifty, 85; at fifty-two, 7; at sixty-three, 112; marriages, 24, 60, 96; bankruptcies, 49, 99; curb membership, 64; divorces, 60, 96; robbed, 83-85; suspended, 100; fisherman, 107; author, 109; suicide, 112
Livermore, Mrs. Jesse L. #2, 64, 84, 96, 103
Livermore, Mrs. Jesse L. #3, 97, 98, 110
Livermore, Jesse L., Jr., Jesse Livermore's son, 64, 83, 102-104, 113
Livermore jewels, 82
Livermore Key, 108, 113; explained, 119ff.
Livermore, Laura (Prouty), Jesse Livermore's mother, 13
Livermore, Paul Alexander, Jesse Livermore's son, 64, 83, 103
Locust Lawn, estate, 64
Loeb, Gerald, market analyst, 108
Longcope, J. W., revenuer, 96
Lord, Jesse, Jesse Livermore's alias, 28, 98

M

Mammoth Oil stock, 69, 71
Meehan, Mike, stock specialist, 94
Mexican Petroleum stock, 66
Mizner, Addison, architect, 87
Mizner Associates, realty company, 82
Mizner, Wilson, playright, 87
Montauk Yacht Club, 105
Montgomery Ward stock, 79
Morgan, J. P., capitalist, 3, 41, 42
Morgantheau, Hon. Henry, Secretary of the Treasury, 86
Morgantheau, Maximillian, investor, 86

N

Neville, D. B., tutor, 103
New York Credit Men's Association, 88

New York Stock Exchange, 48, 55, 67, 88, 93, 101
New York World, The, 46
Noble, Mrs. Harriet Metz, Jesse Livermore's third wife, 96, 97, 98, 110

P

Paine-Webber, stockbrokers, 16
Panic of 1947, 41
Patten Corner, 77
Patten, James A., speculator, 77
Pennsylvania Hotel, 98
Piggly-Wiggly stores and stock, 67, 68
Pirandello, Luigi, author, 113
Plummer, A. Newton, public relations man, 94
Pointers, 53
Police Gazette, periodical, 43, 57
Pool agreement, 65
Pope, Alexander, author, 117
Price, W. W., reporter, 55

R

Radio Corporation of America, RCA, 79
Radio fever, 72
Ranger, charter-fishing boat, 105
Research, 25
Rockefeller, John D., capitalist, 3
Rockefeller, Percy, trader, 94
Rogist, charter-yacht, 104
Roosevelt, President F. D., 93
Roundout School for Scientific Speculation, 77-78
Russell, Lillian, showgirl, 42, 66
Ryan, Thomas F., capitalist, 53, 59, 70

S

Sage, Russell, capitalist, 67, 79
St. Regis Hotel, 60
Saunders, Clarence, grocer, 67, 68

SEC: Securities & Exchange
   Commission, 32, 118
Seneca Copper stock, 65
Sherry-Netherland Hotel, 110, 111
Short-seller, described, 28
Sinclair, Harry F., oil operator, 71
Sinclair Oil Company, 69
Squibb Building, 108
Stork Club, 110
Sweeting, John, charter-boat
   captain, 105

T

Teapot Dome Scandal, 70, 71
Thaw, Harry, assassin, 58
Tierney, J. J. plaintiff, 99
Tight money, 41

U

Union Pacific stock, 33, 34, 35,
   37, 38
United States Navy, 69

Untermyer, Samuel, attorney-at-
   law, 80, 94; cited, 70-71

W

Walker, Mayor James, 88, 93
Wallace, Hon. Henry, Secretary of
   Agriculture, 98, 99, 104
Washburn, Watson, author, 93
Weinberg, Sidney, investment
   banker, 3
Wendt, Dorothy, Mrs. Livermore
   #2, 60
Wheat, 76-81
Whipple, Sherman, civic leader, 57
White, A. S., commodity broker-
   dealer, 76
White, A. S. & Company,
   commodity brokers, 75
White, Stanford, architect, 58
Williston, J. R., stockbroker, 53, 99
Williston, J. R. & Company
   stockbrokers, 54
Wilson, President Woodrow, 55,
   56, 57